Praise for *Fifteen Minutes Outside*

"*Fifteen Minutes Outside* is full of fun, creative ideas that make it easy for busy parents to give their kids much-needed outdoor time in any season. The games, crafts, and projects presented in the book fit perfectly with National Wildlife Federation's Be Out There movement and offer simple ways for families to connect with nature and each other."

—David Mizejewski, naturalist, National Wildlife Federation

"Research now supports what our grandmothers already knew to be true: time spent outdoors is good for our health. In this book, Rebecca P. Cohen offers 365 prescriptions for healthier kids and healthier families."

—Daphne Miller, MD, author of *The Jungle Effect: Healthiest Diets from around the World—Why They Work and How to Make Them Work for You*

"Every family will LOVE getting outside every day with the fun and easy tips in this book! Today, more than ever, we need to preserve our kids' love of the outdoors. Rebecca P. Cohen gives us everything we need to make outside time happen!"

—Whitney Ferré, author of *33 Things to Know About Raising Creative Kids*, www.creativelyfit.com

"Ready to get up and go? Open the pages and start to discover 365 amazing ways to connect and engage with your kids! Keep it in your kitchen, your car, and by your bedside 'cause your family is about to be inspired."

—Pediatric psychologist Dr. Lynne Kenney, author of *The Family Coach Method*

"Every parent wants to keep their kids healthy, but it often feels like a struggle. Rebecca's imaginative and fun ideas help even city dwellers like me take the fifteen-minutes a day challenge."

—Frances Largeman-Roth, RD, senior editor at *Health* magazine and
author of *Feed the Belly: The Pregnant Mom's Healthy Eating Guide*

"Some parents are better than others at getting their kids outside. Of course, one solution is to get rid of TV/computers/video games. With *Fifteen Minutes Outside*, you will discover the best solution is for you to take the lead. Indoors or out, the bonding that comes with shared adventure is priceless. Kids love reading books together or spending time with you in the kitchen. But best of all is going outside together. With this book you will get inspired to make that adventure happen every day, even if it's only for fifteen minutes. This is a lifetime habit your children will thank you for starting—today!"

—Martha Sears, RN, coauthor of *The Baby Book*

"Rebecca P. Cohen reminds us that we can be ourselves with our kids and grow closer as a family starting with *Fifteen Minutes Outside* every day. This is a must-read book for people who want to bring more joy, connection, and fun into their family."

—Mike Robbins, author of *Be Yourself, Everyone Else Is Already Taken*

15 minutes outside

outside

*365 ways to get out of the house
and connect with your kids*

REBECCA P. COHEN

Foreword by Dr. Tererai Trent

Published by Sourcebooks, Inc.
P.O. Box 4410, Naperville, Illinois 60567-4410
(630) 961-3900
Fax: (630) 961-2168
www.sourcebooks.com

Library of Congress Cataloging-in-Publication Data

Cohen, Rebecca P.
  Fifteen minutes outside : 365 ways to get out of the house and connect with
  your kids / by Rebecca P. Cohen.
      p. cm.
  Includes index.
  1. Family recreation. 2. Outdoor recreation. I. Title.
  GV182.8.C64 2011
  790.1'91--dc22

                          2010048512

          Printed and bound in the United States of America.
                VP 10 9 8 7 6 5 4 3 2

To my husband, Bret, whom I met outside,
and to my children, Harmond and Warner,
for whom I play outside every day.

contents

acknowledgments

Writing a first book took as much support as building a business, and there are many people who never hesitated to jump on board this project and believe in it: my book agent, Jessica Papin of Dystel & Goderich Literary Management; my editor, Shana Drehs; the gracious foreword contributor Dr. Tererai Trent; and the fabulous supporting talent of writers like Judy Sternlight and Starla J. King. In addition, thank you to the kids, moms, dads, aunts, uncles, and grandparents who contributed ideas to this book to help future generations and their families live a healthy and happy outdoor lifestyle.

foreword

Fifteen Minutes Outside is a must-have publication for every family, school, and childcare provider who wants to keep kids active year-round. Reading this book is an eye-opener. It is one of the most important books of this decade on how outdoor life can improve the health of families and particularly the health of our children.

According to the U.S. Department of Health and Human Services, the rate of childhood obesity in the United States has more than tripled in the past thirty years. In a society where kids spend more of their time watching TV and playing video games than engaging in creative non-electronic play, Rebecca Cohen's book is timely. Reversing the trend of childhood obesity is an imperative for the well-being of the next generation, and Rebecca offers valuable, sound solutions for creating and keeping healthy families: focusing on loved ones teaming together around simple and fun healthy lifestyle practices such as eating healthy and getting outside every day, together.

When I first met Rebecca, I was struck by her warm personality, and we connected immediately. She distinguished herself immediately as a passionate, enthusiastic, and goal-oriented individual committed to helping transform people by introducing them to healthy lifestyles. I am a strong believer of women who can set goals and visions for a better future, and Rebecca's combination of heart, intellect, and determination promises that positive impact. I am reminded of the African cultural saying: "It takes a village to raise a child." Rebecca shows us that by taking our children, nieces, nephews, and friends outside for fifteen minutes each day, any of us can become that powerful "village" to each other.

Rebecca's message is also about helping each child develop lifelong healthy habits by getting up close and personal with the wonders and bounty of Mother Nature. For example, family time outside provides everyone with invaluable experiences such as growing vegetables, creating a monarch habitat, skipping rocks, attracting hummingbirds, or simply walking in the beautiful sunshine.

This book is jam-packed with sound and doable ideas. Rebecca explains easy outdoor activities for every day of the year, and she gives practical ideas of how to stay (actively) warm in winter and cool in summer.

We're part of a busy society, and perhaps we don't have hours of spare time every day, but we can certainly spare at least fifteen minutes to kick a ball, take a walk, play tag, or watch the clouds race. When we are out of the house and in the fresh air, we are away from distractions, and family members naturally open up to conversations that allow us to learn more about one another. These are the moments that naturally add up to not only an active and healthy lifestyle, but also to closer family relationships.

Just beyond our doorstep is a world waiting to be explored, where we can easily tap into our children's curiosity and follow their lead to uncover what they love so much about the simplest things in life—right in our own neighborhood! I'll also let you in on a little secret: some time outside every day can have a positive impact on any of us, not just the kids.

Every parent, teacher, health practitioner, and civic leader will find Rebecca's book not only inspiring, as she provides practical and innovative strategies to get our children to move more, but also authentic and simple, as she advocates for every person's health and happiness.

Thank you, Rebecca, for your ongoing passion for helping all of us focus on healthier and happier lifestyles. We and our children are grateful.

Dr. Tererai Trent

Dr. Tererai Trent is the founder of Tinogona Consulting Services. As the company's principal evaluator, Dr. Trent has assessed the effectiveness of a wide range of grant programs across the globe. Dr. Trent's personal passion is in women and children's education and transformative resources for families. She resides in California.

introduction

A year ago, for the first time in my life, I made a New Year's resolution and kept it.

I had convinced my two young boys, Harmond and Warner, to drop their computer games and join me for a walk near our home in Virginia. All three of us were bundled up against the bitter cold, and there was a muffled quiet all around us. As we approached a cluster of bare trees, the boys and I discussed how far we could see now that the leaves had fallen. And suddenly, it felt as though the spare landscape and dreary gray sky had come alive with sound and color. Up above, a squirrel was scampering from branch to branch. We flipped a rock over and found squirmy creatures beneath it, and then we continued our walk, crunching along on a fragrant bed of dead leaves. All three of us were enjoying ourselves tremendously. It was exciting to be outside while everyone else was hibernating indoors. Puffs of steam left our mouths whenever we spoke, but we no longer minded the cold. In fact, as we cracked jokes and ran to look at each other's discoveries, we soon became warm enough to peel off a layer or two.

Reflecting on how naturally happy we were whenever we spent time outside, how much we enjoyed each other's company, and how time seemed to slow down in a magical way, I thought, "What if?"

What if I got outside every single day, and what if I could get my kids to come along? It would be easier to pull this off in the middle of summer, but what if we did it all year round, no matter what the weather was like?

At the time, the idea zapped me like a lightning bolt. But really I had been building up to this challenge for a long time.

Three years ago, when my older son was four years old, I took him to a classmate's birthday party at a local park. Gazing up at the huge trees, Harmond asked, "Are we in the forest, Mommy?" I was intrigued but also dismayed by the difference in our perspectives. To me, a forest was an expanse of trees in the wilderness. To my son, this park had the densest concentration of trees that he had ever seen.

My husband and I had demanding corporate jobs, and spending time outside with the kids was limited to precious weekends and rare vacations. Back then, I was always rushing to spend time *inside*—rushing to work, racing down office corridors, eating lunch at my desk between meetings, and then dashing out to pick up my boys so they wouldn't be the last ones at school. On weekdays, it felt as though we were racing through our home rituals—breakfast, dinner, bath, and bedtime routines—and then my husband and I would collapse in front of the TV, exhausted. Our time outside was limited to getting in and out of the car. Family meals out on the patio were our only chance for some fresh air, except for Saturday mornings when I'd tinker in the garden and the kids would play in the sandbox, after which scheduled activities like birthday parties and soccer practice would take over.

Harmond's question about the forest triggered a slow realization for me—I wasn't living my life the way I wanted, and I wasn't giving my family the rich experience of enjoying the outdoors, which was something I had grown up with. We lived in a suburban area known more for its retail shopping mall than green spaces and sidewalks. But that's no excuse—the park we went to for that birthday party was only a mile away.

Time outside means sunshine and fresh air. It means laughter, learning, and unstructured playtime. It means activity and exercise, reflection and conversation, and making time stand still.

I began to spend more time outside with my children, having them help me in the garden. Even on weekdays I encouraged my sons to play outside for a few minutes before we headed to school. We also biked or walked to school whenever possible, rather than driving and waiting in the long drop-off line for cars.

The more I made time for these activities, the closer my family grew, the more fun we had, and the more I learned about myself. Being outside with my kids reduced my stress and allowed me to engage in their sense of curiosity and wonder. It made me realize why I had almost left the financial services industry three years before to pursue landscape design: I wanted to be outside.

I began journaling about my ideal life. And suddenly, I couldn't stop thinking about the logo on a T-shirt that my actress sister proudly wore: "Don't waste your days not doing what you dream to do." With newfound energy, I outlined how I wanted to spend my days.

And then, after talking things over with my husband, I took a leap.

After fifteen years in the corporate world, I left my job and started my own company, Rebecca Plants, LLC (www. rebeccaplants.com), to pursue my passion for gardening and to inspire families to get out and enjoy the natural world. Using my gardening experience and drafting skills from a landscape design course, I started my second career in 2007, designing gardens for people who wanted to do the work themselves. I specialized in year-round color in a garden, including the most fail-proof perennial flowers that return every year, as well as gardening with children.

Over the past three years, my company and my brand have expanded rapidly, giving me a thriving business and a national reputation as an outdoor lifestyle expert. As a spokesmom for the National Wildlife Federation's Be Out There movement, and the host of my own *Get Out of the House* television and radio programs, I am helping millions of families experience daily time outside as a transformative way to spend meaningful time together. I'm doing what I love, promoting an easy and practical outdoor lifestyle for families around the country.

• • •

On that cold, dreary New Year's Day in Virginia, making a silent commitment to get outside with the kids every single day—even for a few minutes—felt like a huge challenge. I wasn't sure how I would pull it off in the middle of a bone-chilling winter. But when I thought about the incredible benefits of outdoor time, I just knew that I was determined to try.

The Benefits of Fifteen Minutes Outside

- Offers great health benefits through fun physical exercise and sunshine
- Redirects children's energies, motivating them to play and explore constructively
- Creates a family stress-relief valve and a way to spend meaningful time together
- Makes life easier for busy parents: play dates outside are hassle-free
- Provides an effortless education in natural science and an appreciation for nature's life cycles

Why Fifteen Minutes Outside Is Good for You

Increasing family time outside is a growing trend, now that we know more about how it can impact our children's health. One in three children is obese. The average child spends more than thirty hours in front of television and electronics a week and gets only four to seven minutes a day of unstructured playtime outside. (The American Academy of Pediatrics recommends at least sixty minutes per day of unstructured playtime outside for children.) Research shows that spending more time outside improves children's concentration in school, lessens aggression, and improves their ability to cooperate. It also increases their levels of vitamin D, which helps to ward off future problems like heart disease and diabetes. And I can tell you from personal experience that it does wonders for adults too.

I am not an expert planner and I'm far from being a serious hiker, biker, or sports player. But I'm great at noticing what makes life easier for busy parents. And redirecting your children's energies, motivating them to play and explore constructively, is always easier outside. I think of outdoor time as a giant relief valve for everyone in the family. Out in the big, natural world, there are tons of possibilities for games, discoveries, and positive interactions.

Loving Those Outdoor Play Dates

Here's a little secret: I take advantage of every opportunity to hold my kids' play dates outside. It's not only about fresh air and sunshine; it's also a fantastic way to entertain my kids and their friends without messing up the house! After sending my sons' friends home covered in mud on a few occasions, I finally started asking their parents to send an extra set of clothes at the start. I also keep on hand a bike or pair of boots that my children have outgrown; I can let their friends borrow them when they come over to have more outside fun together.

I believe an outdoor lifestyle is for anyone. You don't have to be a hiker, camper, environmentalist, or weekend warrior with a kayak on the roof of your car. You don't have to like picking up insects or getting dirty (though you may want to keep towels by the door and lay down a mat for muddy boots). You just have to be open to the idea that you and your kids, or nieces, nephews, or grandkids, can have a richer, healthier, more stimulating life with more fresh air and a closer relationship with the natural world. Frequent outdoor time is not something you master—it's something you simply practice daily for the well-being of your family.

Getting Started

To kick off my family's Fifteen Minutes Outside campaign, I posted a list of fifty outdoor activities right by the back door. I came up with this list for my own kids, but so many friends and followers of *Get Out of the House* were interested in a tool like this that I eventually posted it on my website. It includes family favorites like bubble-blowing, ball-throwing, bird-watching, playing "I spy" or "follow the leader," and planting bulbs and seeds. I set up bins of warm clothing for each of us so we could quickly throw on enough layers to keep us warm, grab something fun to play with, and get outside.

Post the Possibilities!

Post my Rebecca Plants list of "50 Outdoor Activities for Busy Families" (free download from my website, www.rebeccaplants.com) on your back door, or put up your own list of activities based on ideas from this book and ideas from your own family. This will come in handy on hectic days when you can't think straight and you need a quick, easy activity to get the kids outside. Just grab an item or two mentioned in the list (bubbles, binoculars, soccer ball, jump rope, etc.), and head out the door!

The more we went outside, the more the boys came to relish their outdoor time. Each day a new adventure found us as soon as we walked out the door. Something interesting always popped up, and it usually came from my kids. I think you'll find the same is true if you make it a goal to get your family outside on a regular basis.

You might even find yourself inspired—as I was—to start a video and a written journal of your time outside. Mine was nothing fancy; I just kept my small Flip video camera in my pocket to document anything interesting, and then wrote about experiences that particularly touched me. What I noticed over the first dozen one to two minute videos was that regardless of the activity, my kids and I were having a great time. Taking a digital camera on your outings is another good idea; some of those candid shots that capture your family's outdoor adventures will be priceless in the years to come. You might also luck into the perfect shot for next year's holiday card!

Now and Then Outside

If you're a grandparent, aunt, uncle, or family friend, or even a parent who travels for business or has a super-demanding schedule, you might not be the one getting the kids in your life outside on a daily basis.

No problem! Whether your family time is weekly or monthly, or centered around special occasions, *Fifteen Minutes Outside* will give you hundreds of options for creating fun and meaningful outdoor adventures.

Going outside with my family every day has changed my life. Instead of frantically running from task to task, I have learned to use the spaces in my schedule to look around, breathe deeply, and live in the moment. Daily time outside allows my children a chance to learn and play, giving our whole family the opportunity to grow closer with these concentrated and shared experiences.

Thanks to this quality time with my kids, I am still learning and growing in my mid-thirties. Harmond, my older son, is very interested in sports, and I have learned how to play basketball, soccer, and football to keep up with him. I will never be a pro, but in our family attitude is everything. And Warner is fascinated with nature, drawing, and gardening. So with my younger son I get to explore those activities. Each kid is different, and we all have something to teach each other.

The activities in this book are designed to be:

1. Simple. For the most part, you don't need special equipment to have fun outside.
2. Low to no cost. If there is a cost, such as getting a bit out of our comfort zones, the return is greater!
3. Enjoyed every day. Daily outdoor activity keeps your family connected year-round.

I have to confess, sometimes my boys do kick and scream when I ask them to stop what they're doing and come outdoors with me. We all know the limits of our children. There are times when I don't press the issue, especially if we have spent a lot of time outside earlier that day or the evening before. The last thing I want is for my kids to hate being in nature because I pushed too hard. But I take every opportunity to ask myself: can we do that outside? Homework? Breakfast? Dinner? A game? Reading? More often than not, once kids are outside, they'll ask to stay out there longer.

I also learned to enlist the help of my husband. When the boys started to anticipate my drill of deflecting their requests for TV or video games by suggesting time outside, I pulled my husband aside and asked him to initiate some outdoor time as well. This way, the boys would see that it wasn't just a "mommy suggestion," but it was something that was important to both of us. Bret was glad to oblige, luring the boys out with, "Let's go and play catch!" or "I'm going to kick the soccer ball around; see you outside!" Thankfully, outdoor time is something my husband also enjoys; he often gets the boys out without me having to ask, even taking them on long walks and fishing expeditions when I'm out of town.

A Note about Age and Gender

I don't differentiate! I've seen girls and boys enjoy the activities in this book, as young as two and as old as twelve, although the majority of the book is written with preschool to elementary-aged children in mind. Suggest some activities to your child and see which they pick, or proactively try a new activity each day and follow the direction of your child in his or her preferences. I am continuously surprised and impressed with the range of children's interests.

A few minutes of planning is often helpful—and this book will give you hundreds of simple suggestions to map out what to do with your outdoor time. But now and then, I dare you to head out the door with no plan whatsoever. You'll be amazed at what you and the kids discover as you are walking along, and also by the spontaneous activities that spring from your children's imaginations. On days when I don't have a moment to think, I pull out the bubbles. The kids start chasing them and trying to blow them too, and before I know it, they're making up their own activities, like working together to create an obstacle course with our sports equipment, and taking turns barreling through it. That's when I can quietly sneak away to make dinner.

I've organized this book to take you on a yearlong journey, providing monthly chapters that contain 365 simple and creative outdoor activities, one for each day of the year. Each month is filled with suitable tips and suggestions on games, gardening activities, simple science and craft projects, and ways to appreciate wildlife and the natural world. Inspired by my family's first year of getting outside every day, I have also included seasonal essays, drawing on my family's experiences, as well as ideas from parents who shared their stories with me, to inspire you and your family to deepen your connections to nature; dissolve stress; and add more laughter, learning, and family communication to your daily lives. The best way to use *Fifteen Minutes Outside* is to adapt my activities to suit the members of your family. You can read this book front to back, but you can also dip around in it—hopefully for years to come. I hope that this book will inspire your family to explore the outdoors on a regular basis. Getting outside is a free and flexible way to enrich your family—no matter where you live.

Adapting This Book to Your Climate

No matter what your region is like—surrounded by water or out in the desert, flat, mountainous, or filled with skyscrapers—each of us can appreciate the joys of a simple experience outside. And while your local temperatures may not match up to the ones I describe in the book as we move from month to month (and believe me, the weather in Virginia can be anything but consistent in each season), you can easily adapt these activities to suit your particular climate. Since the book is structured by season, you can find activities appropriate for hot, cold, and moderate temperatures, regardless of whether the specific months are the same for you. Most of these activities can be done at any time of year, and for activities that rely on specific temperatures, like vegetable gardening, I have spelled out what temperatures are best for things like planting.

You'll also find a few indoor activities in the book that are outdoor-inspired, for those painfully hot or cold days when you're better off staying home. Mix it up. Try something listed in December during March; you may be surprised how much fun it is!

winter

DO I REALLY HAVE THE POWER TO CREATE MEMORIES EVERY DAY? *YES!*

One bleak and bitter Sunday in January, my two boys were picking on each other in the house. In frustration, my husband turned to me and said, "You're the outdoor expert, what do we do?!" It was still early in my yearlong mission to get the kids outside every day, and I didn't feel like an expert of anything. In desperation, I blurted out, "Let's take a walk." It was thirty degrees out, and the wind chill made it feel much colder. But despite the wind and snow flurries, we bundled up and started walking. Within moments, the boys were laughing at how cold their dad was, and their fight was completely forgotten. We kept walking and came across a wooded path that was begging to be explored. Forty-five minutes later we were almost home, and had even pulled off some layers. We all agreed that we should take nature walks like that more often.

There was something that happened on that frigid walk that turned into an amazing family memory for us. In moving beyond the discomfort of being cold and allowing for the possibility of having a good time together, the four of us had an experience akin to the rare magical moments that happened when we were on vacation. I was eager to initiate more of these meaningful outdoor experiences on a regular basis, no matter how busy we were.

Making the initial decision to get out of the house with my children every day was easy. But the thought of sticking to it, day after day in winter when the daylight hours are shorter and I needed to drum up enthusiasm to step outside in the dark, whether it was morning or evening, felt like a tall order.

For me, outdoor time had to be easy and fun or it wasn't going to happen. So to get us started, I made sure that each of us had toasty warm outdoor gear that fit us properly. I also organized a separate bin of gloves, mittens, scarves, and hats for each member of the family to keep by the back door. This would help us to suit up and get out the door quickly without cries of "Where's my other mitten?"

Good Winter Gear

As long as everyone is warmly dressed (in layers so you can peel them off if you start to heat up!) you can stay out there as long as the kids are happy, active, and entertained. Here are some tips that really work:

- Non-cotton long underwear and socks keep you warm, and snow pants keep your kids from getting wet.

- Waterproof snow boots are great, and so are inexpensive knee-high rain boots with thick socks under them.
- Make sure the elastic liners at the bottom of snow pants are positioned over the tops of boots (not tucked in) to really keep water out.
- When enjoying sports like skiing or snow tubing, consider helmets for the whole family. These can be rented as well as purchased. They are insulated to keep your head warm without a hat, and they are adjustable to fit each head snugly.
- Keep each child's winter gloves, mittens, hats, scarves, etc., in a separate container so it's quick and easy for everyone to suit up and get outside without having to hunt around for missing items. And if you plan to take walks at night and there are roads nearby, pick up reflective gear for yourselves and the dog to keep everyone safe.

I started with short expeditions, thinking if we could duck out for fifteen minutes at a stretch, even that would be an accomplishment. And it was. But the payoff was bigger than I expected because these quick jaunts often led to longer stretches outside. Dressed in warm layers and armed with items like a magnifying glass, shovels, a compass, or a soccer ball, we quickly forgot about the temperature. Winter is a wonderful season to explore the natural world. In many parts of the country, each of the four seasons is so dramatic, especially when you get up close and pay attention.

The way I see it, spending family time outside in the winter is just as important as getting children to eat their vegetables—and in my house, it's a lot easier! (Growing your own certainly helps, but more on that later.) While Harmond and Warner may protest now and then about having to go outside in the ice and snow, within seconds of getting out there they are consuming the outdoor experience voraciously and with far more enthusiasm than when they are faced with something green on their plates. Seeing how well my kids get along when they're out in nature is awe-inspiring. I love the way they relate to each other, and to me, when they're outside. They ask more questions; point out what they see, and ask to stay out longer. As a family, we are naturally happier when we are outside, learning and active together. It doesn't feel like a chore.

You can also use one kid's enthusiasm to inspire another. One February school day, we awoke to beautiful and fast snow flurries. We quickly checked the weather and school closings to make sure we still had to get ready for school. We learned that it would get warmer later in the day and the snow would be gone when the kids got home. I said, "Who's coming outside with me to walk the dog and play in the snow?" My younger son started getting ready but my older son didn't budge. The snow was barely covering the grass but it *was* covering the driveway. "Warner, why don't you get in the sled and I'll pull you around while I walk Sampson?" "Yeah!" he replied. So I pulled him around on our usual dog-walking route. When we got home, Warner asked if he could shovel the driveway. "Sure!" I said (not going to argue with that). I went inside to get breakfast ready and found Harmond playing with his Nintendo DS. "Harmond, Warner and I had a great time outside. I pulled him on the sled while I walked the dog!" "Really?!" He was slightly excited. I said, "He's shoveling the driveway now. Why don't you join him? I don't want you to miss out on the fun." When Harmond protested that he didn't want to wear his snow pants, I told him his snow boots, coat, and gloves would be enough. He had loads of fun out there, riding his scooter in the snow and having a shoveling race with his brother. I brought out hot chocolate and a warm muffin and served it to them on the porch. Everyone was totally satisfied with making the most of our brief wintry wonderland. We were a little rushed getting out the door, but we made it to school safely and on time.

Can you think of other indoor activities that might be fun to try outside, even in the winter? My boys get a big kick out of eating outside and love our winter picnics. In fact, as they got used to their extended outdoor time, they started clamoring for more outdoor breakfasts before school. They also invited their friends over for outdoor play dates. They liked going on nature walks when their friends came over to play, and their friends started asking for the nature walks! And, after one (secretly harrowing) local hike with six kids, when I forgot to go over the rules in advance (like making sure they could see me at all times rather than running too far ahead), I made sure to give my own kids, as well as their friends, some basic safety rules up front at the start of each expedition.

Ask your children to point out things that are more fun in winter than in summer. For example, according to my boys, our backyard play set doesn't have spiders on it when the temperature drops, and the kids can play follow the leader on logs in the woods without walking into spiderwebs. And looking through the bare trees we are able to see the most incredible sunrises, sunsets, and clear, starry skies.

I learned that setting up good habits at the start of the year—like spending more time out-of-doors even when it's cold—makes things much easier as the year progresses. Even when we're inside, we're thinking of ways to enjoy outdoor-inspired activities, whether we're learning about the seasonal changes and wildlife in books or creating crafts with items we've collected from outside. As the landscape slowly thaws, you'll be delighted at how skilled your family has become at finding more creative ways to enjoy the outdoors and your time together. And the rewards year-round are tremendous.

Organize Those Outside Toys

Just when I thought organizing everyone's shoes by the door was difficult enough, I realized we have lots of outside toys, even if simple items, to arrange. Whichever method you choose, likely the most important thing is that the kids know where to put the toys back and can do so themselves. For example, at a child's

level you can have cubes or a shelving unit with baskets or clear plastic tubs for smaller items like chalk,
bubbles, jumping ropes, and their gardening tools. If
you are very organized, like I've seen in schools, you
can tape a picture of the item with the word underneath. I like using buckets for similar items (e.g., smaller balls all together). Up high (for me) I have a shelf
by the door dedicated to sunscreen, bug spray, and a
first-aid kit. But most of our outside toys are in an inexpensive black metal organizer for sports equipment,
which can work in a closet or garage. Even if you don't
have sports equipment, the hooks and bins are helpful;
as long as the toys are hung up on a hook or in one of
the bins, they are considered tidy.

january

Bundle up and start the New Year
with fresh expeditions and dreams!

The twinkling lights have been taken down, the holidays are behind us, and everyone's talking about New Year's resolutions for healthier living, smarter spending, closer relationships, and less stress. What are you hoping for this year? Start walking in the mornings or evenings to mull it over and bring your loved ones along. Share your thoughts with your kids and ask them what they'd like to accomplish in the months ahead. What are their dreams and hopes for the year?

Getting outside every day was my resolution for the New Year. More important to me than watching the pounds drop or the bank account grow, it was about gaining back beautiful time that I had squandered in previous years by hibernating until my spring bulbs began to bloom. My older son wanted more travel time with Mom and Dad and my younger son wanted to visit lots of water parks. We all agreed that it would be an exciting year with the upcoming adoption of our first dog; we would take good care of him, and he'd give us lots of love in return—not to mention plenty of outdoor time! You too can set the stage for a great year by talking with your kids about what they are looking forward to doing with you.

January Activities

1. EXPLORE AS A NATURALIST

I once read an article that a naturalist has the ability to find wonder in the ordinary. Find an easy outdoor location near your home to observe gradual changes in the natural world—whether it's a wooded path near your home or a city park. Bring along binoculars or a magnifying glass, as well as pocket guides to the local birds and plants. Each time you go there, make a fresh discovery—whether it's a bug frozen into a puddle, a piercing bird call, a squirrel performing death-defying leaps, or the delicious smell of pine needles. Remind the kids to use all of their senses. Every time my family takes a nature walk, we notice something new.

Look It Up!

When kids explore the natural world, they're bound to ask a million questions. Sometimes you'll know the answers, and sometimes you'll be stumped. If you draw a blank when they grill you about photosynthesis, the eating habits of eagles, or how rocks are formed, get them excited about looking up the answers once you're back home. This is a great, lifelong habit to cultivate—it makes learning fun and rewarding.

2. HAVE A SUNRISE BREAKFAST

Make a piping hot breakfast (hot cereal or warm muffins work well, and so does hot milk or cocoa), bundle up, and enjoy an early-morning picnic outside on a blanket. In January, if you time it right, your family can catch a sunrise while you eat. Watching the sun rise and set is always great, but it's extra magical when the trees are bare, giving you greater visibility.

3. ENJOY THE SNOW TOGETHER

When those soft, white flakes are floating down, why not join in the childlike fun? Build a snowman, go sledding, make snow angels in the yard, or carve a sculpture in the snow with a big spoon or kitchen spatula. When I was a teenager, a boy who had a crush on my sister carved a life-sized alligator in our front yard. You and your kids can make smaller interpretations of their favorite creatures. Remember that fun, rather than perfection, is the name of the game! And whatever snowy activity you pick, don't forget to cap it off with some hot cocoa or soup when you get back home. Or scoop up some fresh snow in a bowl, bring it home, add maple syrup, and enjoy a natural frozen treat!

4. GIVE YOUR CHILDREN'S IMAGINATIONS A WORKOUT

While your kids are outside enjoying sunshine and physical exercise, why not have them exercise their imaginations as well? Encourage them to climb a hill and pretend it's Mount Everest, build a fort with tree branches, or prepare a pretend feast using leaves as plates and wild berries as the main course. Ask them about stories they are reading at school and at home, and join them in acting out their favorite parts. Mary Pope Osborne's Magic Tree House series is perfect for this, but there are hundreds—even thousands—of great children's books (and movies and even video games) to draw on. Folk tales like "The Three Little Pigs," "Goldilocks and the Three Bears," and "The Gingerbread Man," or children's favorite board books such as *The Very Hungry Caterpillar* by Eric Carle or *We're Going on a Bear Hunt* by Michael Rosen and illustrated by Helen Oxenbury are a great place to start.

What is Important to Your Family?

What do you wish you could do more of outside every day? Ask this question of each member of your family. Don't forget yourself! The answers are a great way to know what is important in how you spend your time. You may hear some great ideas or simple ways that you can work some fresh air into your routine.

5. REINVENT YOUR COMMUTE

Instead of driving your kids to school or putting them on a bus or subway to get there, try biking with them or walking them to school. If the distance is moderate, this can be a very enjoyable expedition—every morning or just now and then. The kids will enjoy this extra family time with you, and they will also enjoy a little more outdoor time before their school day begins.

6. KEEP A NATURE JOURNAL

Kids have a natural tendency to pick up interesting objects and to make wonderful observations and stories about what they find. Invite yours to start a nature journal or scrapbook to keep track of their favorite moments and discoveries outside. They can focus on what interests them the most—plants, animals, daring adventures, funny stories—describing things in colorful pictures and words. Maybe they will want to snap outdoor photos to include in the journal. If your family has a video camera, you can also make a simple outdoor documentary to share with friends and family.

7. IMPROVISE A HOCKEY GAME

Make an ice puck by pouring an inch of water in a mug and leaving it outside overnight. Or select a piece of loose ice you find outside, or even a tennis ball, for the puck. Sticks in your backyard or lying on the ground in your local park can become hockey sticks. Your kids can knock the homemade puck around on the sidewalk. In a pinch, my kids have also used their baseball bats as hockey sticks, making sure to keep them low to the ground.

8. EXAMINE THE ICE AND THEN TURN IT INTO A MASTERPIECE!

Examine the ice outside. Look at the layers, bubbles, leaves, sticks, and other items that add to the texture of it. My kindergartner recently remembered his science lessons while we scrutinized a piece of ice in our yard. "Mom, did you know that ice is a solid, which turns to water—a liquid—when it melts, and when it disappears into air it's a gas!" After you have examined the ice, why not turn it into a work of art? Using paint brushes and homemade watercolors (water mixed with food coloring) have your kids make a painting right on a piece of ice. Younger kids will enjoy using spray bottles, each filled with a different color of paint (water and food coloring), to create an abstract painting on the ice.

9. GET TO KNOW A TREE

Close your eyes and have your child lead you to a tree. Use your senses—touch, smell, and hearing—to learn all you can about your tree. The bark will have its own texture, tiny buds may be forming on branches, and the trunk will be easy or hard to get your arms around. With your eyes still closed, have your child lead you back to where you started. Open your eyes and try to find your tree. Now it's your child's turn!

10. GO ON A SCAVENGER HUNT!

Give your kids a magazine and have them cut out five things that they may be able to find outside. Use a glue stick or tape to adhere the pictures to a piece of paper, give the kids a plastic bag, and let them search in the yard or park for the items! You can vary the activity by asking the children to find one, two, or three of each item based on what you think is available and how long you want them to look.

11. TRAIN A NEW GENERATION OF EXPLORERS

Explore north, east, south, and west with your kids. Watch one morning as the sun comes up (east) and in the evening to see where the sun goes down (west) and then let your kids decide which direction to follow on your next walk. You can buy them a pocket compass for less than $10. To practice the four cardinal directions, have your kids draw a map of your yard, your neighborhood, a nature trail, or a local playground. They can use a compass or the position of the sun to determine where north, east, south, and west are located. You can also make a treasure hunt. Hide a special treat outside, such as a younger child's favorite toy or a small bag of change for older kids. Draw a map to the treasure (using the four directions) and challenge the kids to follow it.

12. STARGAZE

Step outside for a short walk after dinner. There is so much to see at night in the winter sky. If you have a telescope, bring it along. And if the moon is full, see if you can find your moon shadows. Here are a couple of books for budding young astronomers: *Stars: A Guide to the Constellations, Sun, Moon, Planets and Other Features of the Heavens* by Herbert S. Zim, Robert H. Baker, and Mark R. Chartrand, illustrated by James Gordon Irving; and *The Kids Book of the Night Sky* by Ann Love and Jane Drake, illustrated by Heather Collins.

13. CREATE WITH OR COUNT PINECONES

Head out to look for pinecones; don't forget to look up in the pine trees as well as down on the ground. Hunt for special pinecones to put in a basket in the house, make a mobile, or dip them in paint and make fun designs on paper. Don't want to collect the pinecones? Find a pine tree and count how many pinecones you see. Decide together how to remember where your pine tree is located. Then, return to your tree every week to see if there are more pinecones, or if the pinecones on the branches have grown bigger!

14. ENCOURAGE BUDDING ARTISTS

Bring a notepad and colored pencils along on your next outing and invite your kids to draw what they see. When you're back home, help them to write down a story that goes with the picture. If you keep a pad, pencils, and crayons in the car, your kids can sketch the changing landscape whenever you're on a family trip.

15. HAVE FUN IN THE LIGHT SNOW

When there's not enough snow for sledding or snowman-building, your kids can still have a blast with a light dusting of powdery flakes. Using a stick, a wooden spoon, a push broom, or a shovel, you can make wonderful designs in the snow on a flat surface like a driveway or a sidewalk. If there's enough snow to make a couple of good snowballs, have your kids store them in the freezer. Then, in the middle of summer, they can take the snowballs outside to show their friends!

16. IMAGINE YOU'RE A SQUIRREL...

If you could climb like a squirrel, where would you go? Invite your kids to pretend to be an animal that they see on a regular basis and have them explore the outdoor world as that creature. Is the animal fast or slow? Does it jump or fly? Where would it find food? Where would it live?

17. MEASURE AND TRACK THE WINTER PRECIPITATION

Make rain gauges from plastic bottles. Cut a two-liter plastic bottle in half. Place two or three small rocks in the bottom half to weigh it down. Then, turn the top half of the bottle upside-down and place it in the bottom half so it acts as a funnel to capture precipitation. Place your newly made rain gauge on the ground, then take a yardstick and mark it with a permanent marker each inch. Or you can use yardsticks to measure the snowfall. Have each of you take a guess as to how much it rained or snowed before you check the gauge!

18. HONOR HISTORY

Martin Luther King Jr. Day falls in January and, for most of us, it's a school holiday. Why not participate in the nationwide King Day of Service? Research local projects your family could participate in, like volunteering at a homeless shelter or a center for the elderly, participating in a stream cleanup, or getting involved in a school-related project (check out www.mlkday.gov). One recent January 21st, a local organization near me had a record number of volunteers, many of whom were families. One hundred and sixty volunteers picked up over 170 bags of trash! If you volunteer in the morning, you can also take your kids for an outdoor picnic near a historic civil rights or service landmark to talk about the importance of the day.

19. SEARCH FOR ANIMAL TRACKS

Take a walk outside—in the park, the yard, or the woods—and see what kinds of tracks you can find. Sometimes the tracks you find may be your own. How can you tell? Compare your footprints to those you may find on a trail or a path. Are there other signs that animals are around? A bird's nest? A hole at the bottom of a tree? Animal scat? Broken nut shells?

20. HOST AN INFORMAL NEIGHBORHOOD ACTIVITY

Invite the neighborhood kids over for tag, muffins, and hot cocoa on a Saturday morning (or, if they are older, soccer or touch football). It's fun to see how long they want to play outside, and it starts the day off right for everyone. Those not into group play can warm up with jumping jacks and jumping rope.

Explore the Plant Life Cycle with Your Kids!

Buy some herb seeds and plant them in a cardboard egg carton with soil in the egg-slots. Place it on a sunny windowsill and have the kids water it daily by squeezing a moist cotton ball or paper towel over each egg-slot. You can also collect the seeds from your apples and oranges—my younger son loves this! Press the seeds into lightly moistened cotton balls (one to two drops of water), place them into zip lock bags, and tape the bags to a sunny window. It's a science lab right in your own home! If you're lucky, you might be able to transplant some of these little science projects (at least the herbs) outside in the spring.

21. STAGE A FLASHLIGHT DRAMA OUTSIDE

If you have flashlights and glow sticks at home, your kids can stage a fantastic outdoor display after the sun goes down. My boys and their friends love running around with their flashlights, crossing the light like swords, or creating designs with their beams of light. Everyone pitches in on the sound effects too.

22. GO ON A BIRD WATCHING EXPEDITION

Bundle up with a blanket and a thermos of hot cocoa and wait for the birds to forget that you're there. Count the number of different birdcalls you hear and the number of different birds that you see. Take a sketchpad and have the kids draw their favorite birds and afterward look up what type of birds they may be. In January, we've seen woodpeckers, sparrows, doves, bluebirds, chickadees, and ducks.

23. RIDE THE BUS OR TRAIN SOMEWHERE

Let's get real—kids love buses and trains! So why not organize a trip that involves public transportation? The final destination could be a museum, a bookstore, or even a favorite restaurant. The big adventure will be getting there and back on a train or a bus.

24. VISIT THE PLAYGROUND AFTER A SNOWFALL

Everything looks different after a snowfall. Playgrounds, for instance, can be a magical place when covered in white powder. Keeping an eye out for safety issues, let your kids enjoy the snowy playground. My girlfriend with toddler-triplets took her kids to the snowy playground and made a ramp of snow at the base of the slide. While they were too young to go sledding, the slide let her family simulate a real snowy hill in a safe place where the ground was cushioned with a soft, rubbery surface.

25. TRY SOME RACING GAMES

Most kids love to run and let off steam. Direct all that kid energy onto the grass and have them hop like kangaroos, frogs, and rabbits, or run in a big circle like bats or flying squirrels. Have them race to different trees (a friend of mine calls this her family's version of tree-hugging), or set up a relay race with your kids and their friends during a play date. For a relay, you could announce a different type of animal action with each stage of the race. High fives and giggles are the only prizes you need!

26. HAVE AN ART SHOW OF ICICLES

My kids couldn't wait to show me the icicles they collected from around the outside of our house. Like snowflakes, each was different, and my older son proudly described where he found each of them and how each was different from the rest. We had fun talking about how icicles are created, one drop of water freezing at a time.

27. CREATE THE WINTER OLYMPICS

If there is enough snow on the ground, create tubing, luge, and toboggan runs. How do you tell the difference? According to my kids, each track is designed to give you a unique experience. For tubing, scoop a curved path down the slope with a shovel to make an easy path for the tube. The luge track is a straight downhill shot, and the toboggan run should follow a winding path, built for a flat, straight sled (on which you lie down). We don't have a huge hill or a lot of space in our yard, but we have just enough incline to pick up speed and make it through our runs. Parents definitely need to help with this one, so it is a great family activity. No snow? How about skating? If you don't have ice skating nearby, your kids can simulate the Olympic skating events on roller skates or roller blades.

28. SET UP AN INDOOR CAMPSITE

Let's face facts—sometimes it's too cold and nasty to enjoy a long stretch of outdoor time. So why not let your kids re-create the outdoors, right in your living room or basement? They can drape a blanket over two chairs to make a tent, build a "campfire" with blocks, and bring in a snack of made-in-the-microwave s'mores (put a marshmallow and a piece of chocolate between two graham crackers and microwave on high for ten seconds). Talk about the real camping adventure that you want to have as soon as it warms up.

29. THINK BIG THOUGHTS

A female entrepreneur once told me that when she was a kid, her mom would tell her to sit under a small tree and have small thoughts, and then sit under a big tree and think big thoughts. Try it with your kids, and have fun discovering what each of you thinks about.

30. PLAY FOLLOW THE LEADER AND "INVESTIGATE"

"I *love* investigating!" exclaimed my five-year-old when he took me outside one cold weekday night to explore our yard. "What's investigating?" I asked. Flabbergasted, he said, "Investigating means finding stuff, Mom." Let your kids play Sherlock Holmes, exploring mysteries in the natural world with a magnifying glass. If it's dark out, bring a flashlight. Shining a thin spotlight on one area at a time can lead to magical discoveries of night insects, tiny holes where woodpeckers have searched for bugs, lichen on rotting wood, berries that animals may eat, or heavy thicket where birds may live.

31. DREAM ABOUT YOUR GARDEN

In many parts of the United States, January is too cold for outdoor gardening—we're jealous of those of you in

Southern California and Florida right about now! But you can still dream and plan for the spring. Take a walk in your outdoor space together. What will you and your children plant when the weather warms up? Ask your kids what they like best. Berries? Flowers? A place to sit and look at the garden? Keep a running list of your favorites. It will help you decide what to plant when the weather warms up. Inside, get out the crayons and colored pencils and have your children draw what they want your garden to look like. Vegetables, trees, shrubs, flowers? There is no wrong answer. You can post your colorful dream gardens while you wait for spring bulbs to poke through.

february

Resist hibernating even on the darkest days.

We've held on for so long and it's still dark out there, still cold. Don't give up; get more creative. Put on more layers and always try to say yes to your kids when they ask to go outside. I've learned the hard way that asking them to wait while you put dinner in the oven doesn't always fly. Ten minutes later and they may be involved in an indoor activity (like my seven-year-old playing with his video games, for example). And then—good luck reigniting that enthusiasm!

Because February can be particularly dreary and cold, it is helpful to make a habit of bringing what you notice outside into your discussions. For example, when you step outside, show your kids something beautiful or interesting. Ask them to tell you what they see, smell, and hear. If you don't notice anything special right away, make a game of it. See who can be the first to point out something remarkable. Make this game a part of your routine and see if February feels different than it has in the past.

February Activities

1. CREATE ART AND ARCHITECTURE WITH ICE

Fill ice cube trays with water and set them outside to freeze overnight. Have your kids build a city outside with the ice bricks (or build the city inside, if it's too cold out). You can also freeze interesting shapes from mugs, bowls, and pans—anything that holds water!

2. ON GROUNDHOG DAY, WATCH FOR WILDLIFE

On February 2nd, Groundhog Day, Punxsutawney Phil in western Pennsylvania has a tradition of "predicting" six more weeks of winter if he sees his shadow. Make a tradition of watching for wildlife where you live. The National Wildlife Federation's Wildlife Watch is a national nature-watching program created for people of all ages. You can look up pictures of animals to look for by region of the United States at www.nwf.org/WildlifeWatch.

3. PLAN A MONARCH WAY STATION

Here's a great family project: You can help preserve and protect the monarch butterfly through Monarch Watch (www.monarch watch.org/waystations). This organization will send you a kit to plant butterfly-friendly seeds in early spring, but now is the time to get started as some of the seeds need to be "cold-stratified" or exposed to cold temperatures (e.g., put seeds in between two moist paper towels in a closed plastic bag in the refrigerator) for six weeks and then sprouted in soil indoors before transplanting them outside when temperatures are in the seventies.

A Note about Wintry Snacks

I mention hot cocoa, warm cider, muffins, oatmeal, and s'mores a lot in the colder month activities. Why? Because these treats are part of my family's special memories in getting outside when it is cold. I even take mini marshmallows in a plastic bag to the ski slope or tubing park so that our hot cocoa has that extra sprinkle of fun on top. Your family may have other traditions; the important thing is that you find what makes special memories for your family and you have fun!

4. MAKE A CABIN-FEVER PREVENTION KIT

Place a bag near the door and fill it with flashlights, battery-operated glow sticks, a thermos for hot cocoa, and pocket guides to wildlife and the night sky. The next time your kids are going stir-crazy at night, take them out for an evening walk. Your kids can watch their "smoky" breath under a flashlight. Hold a flashlight under your chin and breathe out. See how your warm breath swirls around in the cold air! Your family will have fun exploring the natural world from a different perspective, and the lights will keep you safe and on the right path.

5. GET MOVING! YES SIR! YES MA'AM!

You're only cold if you're not moving! Pretend you're at boot camp and jog up and down the sidewalk together, or venture further if you'd like. Try chanting to get you in line: recite an oldie but goodie ("I don't know but I've been told…") or make up one of your own. "Get those knees up!

Faster, private!" See how much silly fun you can have, and how warm you can get.

6. HEAT UP AN OUTDOOR SNACK

When it's cold, I love keeping muffin mix and hot cocoa at the ready for a snack outside. Watching the steam billow up from a cup of hot milk, cocoa, or hot cereal or muffins still makes my kids smile with delight! The kids can pile on their winter gear and play outside while I heat up their snacks, and then they are warm enough to sit on the stoop and enjoy it. Best of all, if we have somewhere to head out to, the boys are all ready when it's time to go!

We're Not Always Outside

After the kids are done playing in the snow and ready to come in, here are some outdoor-inspired ideas for inside:

- Balloon volleyball is great exercise and all you need is to blow up a balloon!
- Kicking a soft soccer ball through a play tunnel keeps the balls on the floor and away from the furniture.
- Use individually wrapped toilet paper for building towers and knocking them down.
- Do you need a change of pace? Head to the rec center for some indoor swimming, tennis, or racquetball.
- Dance to your favorite songs.
- Find inspiration for a craft with objects that you bring inside, such as leaves, seed pods, or sticks. Or sit

with paper, crayons, and paint by the window and create what you see.

7. PLAY THE GAME "WHAT'S BEAUTIFUL TODAY?"

Some days are so dreary, you find yourself wishing for even a little brightness and beauty. Trust me, even in February, it's out there—but sometimes your family has to work together to find it. Bring in everyone's perspectives and head out to find something that is beautiful. Each person's job is to look until they find something in nature that they like and to share why. For example, "Today, the green moss at the bottom of this tree is beautiful. I like it because the color is so bright compared to what surrounds it."

8. BRUSH OFF THE LAYERS: WINTER ARCHAEOLOGY

Pick an interesting outdoor spot (in your yard or a local park) and search beneath the surface like Indiana Jones, winter-style. First, bundle up with lots of layers, head to toe, to stay warm. Warm hats, gloves, and socks are a must. Remember how Indiana always brushes off thick dust to uncover his treasure? Head out with a dustpan broom to sweep off layers of frost, snow, or dirt to see what is hidden beneath; if you don't have a broom, brushing off layers with your gloves will do.

9. TAKE A WINTER BIKE OR SCOOTER RIDE

With a hat under a helmet and gloves keeping your fingers warm, riding a bike or scooter in the cold can be just as fun as any other time of the year. As long as it's not too snowy or icy, ride around your neighborhood for fifteen minutes and you'll be warmed up and ready for another activity outside!

10. HAVE A SHOVELING RACE

As soon as the snow starts falling, my kids grab the shovels and are ready to race from one end of the driveway or sidewalk to the other, seeing who can scoop up the snow the fastest. Inevitably, they get tired just in time for the heaviest snow to accumulate for Mom and Dad. But a shoveling race is a great way to blow off some steam and warm them up to stay out longer.

11. PLAY WHATEVER OUTDOOR GAME YOUR CHILD WANTS TO PLAY

Sometimes it's hard for me to enthusiastically say yes when I am asked to play a game outside that I never liked growing up. I have to confess, it's a big list: football, baseball, four square—really most sports! But take on the challenge; invite your child, grandchild, niece, or nephew outside and tell them you'll play whatever they want to play for fifteen minutes. You never know, you may just end up wanting to play a lot longer!

12. BE AN ARCTIC EXPLORER

On some days, your neighborhood turns into what feels like the arctic tundra, with frigid wind blowing across the frozen landscape. Go ahead and wince a little—then bundle up and get outside to see if you can take it. Make sure your faces are protected with scarves or fleece neck-warmers that can safely go up over your nose. If your kids have ski goggles or sunglasses, it's a great time to use them to keep the blowing snow out of their eyes. Explore the neighborhood together. Dig a shelter in the snow or lean fallen branches around a tree to create a shelter from the "arctic" winds.

13. MAKE A SNOWBALL VOTIVE

As a child, my friend Tina from Norway would stack circles of snowballs in a cone or evergreen shape, with space in each snowball for a votive candle. She would place votive candles in her tower and her parents would light them at night for a beautiful winter display. Whether you create a twinkling tower or a single snowball votive, it's definitely a beautiful way to light up a cold February night. Of course, remember to keep an eye on your candles and blow them out before bed.

14. TAKE A VALENTINE'S DAY WALK DOWN MEMORY LANE

One great way to share your love on Valentine's Day is to lead your loved ones on a walk and show them the places that mean the most to you. Take the kids to an outdoor spot that holds meaningful family history. The parents of a friend of mine fell in love while walking across the Brooklyn Bridge together, so that bridge now holds special meaning for the whole family. You can also flip it around and let the kids lead. My children took their grandparents on a walk from my parents' house to the overpass where they loved to look at trains. The tour continued to the footbridge over a creek where they race sticks, and to the park rose garden where—in warmer weather—the fragrant flowers would return. In each spot the children told their grandparents why they liked coming to that spot with them.

15. SLIDE OR ROLL WITH A POOL RING

Blow-up plastic pool rings (also known as inner tubes or donuts) get used in our yard all year long. They are great as extra cushions when rolling down hills, and they can also serve as inner tubes for sledding. Dig one out of the closet and you'll be buying more later in the year at the local discount store's end-of-summer sale!

16. GUESS THE TEMPERATURE

On the way to school in the morning, my husband started asking my boys to guess the temperature. Over time, the children started to associate a temperature reading with how it felt outside. I found an old outdoor thermometer at a garage sale and now the children have learned to read the temperature, which makes the game even more fun. Knowing the temperature has helped them to gauge how much they need to bundle up.

17. ROLL THE BIGGEST SNOWBALL EVER

In my experience, if you roll a snowball to a certain size, it is destined to become part of a snowman. Not so, according to my seven-year-old! In fact, it is possible to continue rolling the snowball for the sheer gratification of rolling the biggest snowball ever. What makes this activity wonderful for the whole family is that you all have to work together to keep the ball rolling, and man, it is great exercise!

Create an Early Spring Indoors

Forcing blooms takes a little patience but it's a delightful experiment to try with your kids. Go out and find a shrub or a tree that ordinarily flowers in the spring, such as forsythia, pussy willow, quince, or magnolia. How to find one? Look for branches with plentiful buds (by mid-February many early bloomers should already have these tiny buds—look for plump ones). Cut one- to two-foot lengths with pruning shears and bring them inside. Place the branches in water (room temperature) and away from direct sunlight and heat. Replace the water one or two times a week, have the kids spray mist on the branches, and cut an inch off the stems each time the water is replaced. In one to three weeks, the cuttings will bloom and you'll have an early indoor spring!

18. WATCH THE CLOUDS RACE

When you're making snow angels with your child or you just happen to be lying on the grass looking up at the sky, pick two or more clouds and watch them race. Select another cloud and count how long it takes to reach the finish line. Are all clouds traveling at the same speed?

19. DANCE OUTSIDE!

Whatever music you like, that music is portable. Why not rock out in the yard? Any day is a reason to celebrate and have a good time together—and giggle too—as a family. Head outside with some tunes and show your family your best moves.

20. CELEBRATE THE PRESIDENTS

George Washington and Abraham Lincoln didn't have TVs. Celebrate the presidents by experiencing the outdoor hobbies of their era. George Washington was a planter or farmer. Visit a local farm to see the animals. Or imagine and do what Abraham Lincoln's children might have liked to do in winter outside: Hula-hoop? Build a snowman? Feed the birds? If you'd like to learn about some games from the 1800s, look up an article on the Internet called "Games Children Play(ed)" by Stanley Ransom.

21. "OFF-ROAD" IT

Without vines, tall grasses, and brush blocking your way, it's easier in winter to find a new walking or biking path together. Instead of taking your usual path, go "off-road" as a family to explore a new area or find a new way home. When my kids were two and four, we didn't have many mature trees in our neighborhood, so we'd off-road frequently to look for the tallest trees we could find.

22. CLIMB A TREE

Of course, it's great to climb a tree any time of year. But finding a good climbing tree in February can be a reason to get outside, and sometimes we need just that: a reason to get us out the door. Who doesn't love to climb a tree? We don't have a climbing tree in our yard, so we have to go looking for them. Local parks and historic sites can have great old trees perfect for climbing with a grown-up's help. And it doesn't matter if you can't go higher than the first branch. Hanging from a lower branch or perching on top of it can be a lot of fun.

23. CREATE A SOCCER TRAINING CAMP

You don't need a real soccer ball and you don't need to stick to the official rules (my seven-year-old might disagree, but no matter). Pick a target together that will serve as your goal (in between two trees or two items from your closet will do). Then make up drills to reach the goal: pass the ball to each other, dribble around cones (or buckets or sticks—whatever you have), or kick it past a goalie. High five and celebrate your team's victory!

24. TRACK AN ANIMAL

In January, I mentioned finding tracks, but what about following them? It sounds slightly scary and exciting at the same time. My five-year-old and I followed some tracks in the deep snow that led around a path; they looked like small boot prints. After following the tracks into the woods we came upon a spot where the snow was cleared and there was lots of deer scat. That's when we realized that the tracks must have been from a herd of deer! We couldn't wait to trek back home and tell the rest of the family about our adventure.

25. COLD INDOORS? HEAD OUTSIDE AND PLAY TAG

Do something crazy with your kids. Shout, "Let's play tag!" and see how fast you can all bundle up and start chasing each other outside. It may be so much fun that you'll be surprised how long you stay out there. Best of all, coming in from the cold always feels fantastic, and you won't be cold indoors anymore!

26. PLAY WINTER GOLF

In most places, golf courses may not be open in winter, but yours can be open all year round. If you have a yard, a driveway, or a park nearby, you can create a crazy mini-golf course using tipped-over plastic or metal cups. You can even carve out ramps and holes for the golf balls in the snow. No kid-sized golf clubs? Just make your own with a stick inside a stuffed sock inside a shoe.

27. TRY SOME SUNNY SCIENCE WITH NEWSPAPER

My Uncle Denny taught me another cool way to watch a seed sprout on a windowsill. Take a glass or clear cup, put some crumpled newspaper inside, and place a seed or two against the inside of the glass (some good seeds to use are pea, bean, or sunflower). Keep the newspaper moist and, over a week or two, watch the seed sprout! Transfer into a pot with soil (with a drainage hole and saucer underneath to catch water) when the plant outgrows its glass.

28. LEARN A WINTER SPORT AS A FAMILY

There are so many to choose from beyond the sledding that you can do in your neighborhood: downhill skiing, snowboarding, cross-country skiing, snowshoeing—and there are probably more. Find out from friends which winter sports they enjoy as a family and get the inside scoop on how to learn inexpensively. For example, you may be able to rent ski equipment for less at a local shop than it would cost to rent similar equipment at the mountain. Or a local ski resort may have discounts for first-time skiers. If you try a new sport and your family is hooked, many local shops offer discounted used equipment and trade-up programs for equipment as your kids grow.

spring

PRACTICE THE ART OF GENTLE PERSUASION AND LEARN TO FOLLOW THEIR LEAD

Last spring, while the flowers bloomed and bright green leaves were bursting from the trees, my kids were not yet volunteering to run outside and play every day. Even though I kept our snow gear by the door (gradually adding umbrellas, boots, and other warm, waterproof gear), I still had to push myself to lead them outside every day. Fortunately, by encouraging my children to view their outdoor family time as something special, just for them, I reconnected with my own enthusiasm. I started noticing what the kids enjoyed doing, and making suggestions that suited each child. Or sometimes I simply asked, "What would be fun to do together outside right now?"

Even now, it usually falls on me to make suggestions of activities that will motivate my boys to step outside, and I have to stay on my toes for those times when they finish one activity and the easiest choice for them is to go back inside. But I promise you, coming up with ideas gets easier over time. The more I observe about my children's preferences and latest discoveries, the easier it is to propose new games or adventures when enthusism for a particular activity starts to fade.

I also learned to follow my kids' leads whenever they had something to offer, letting them initiate where our next outdoor adventure would take us. The more I was able to look at the world through the eyes of my children—noticing a tadpole, hundreds of droplets on a tree after a rainstorm, or how happy they were riding their bikes around the neighborhood—the more I knew that I was doing the right thing for them and me. And I stopped feeling anxious about whether I was doing "well" at getting the boys outside every day. Our brief, local adventures continue to be very rewarding, and they've led to some amazing displays of childhood creativity and curiosity—two things I am eager to foster in my children.

One afternoon in particular stands out in my mind. My seven-year-old was on spring break while his brother was in day care and instead of asking for TV-time, Harmond asked me to play "store" with him. We arranged some of our recent food purchases on the counter and my customer "purchased" the groceries from me, paying with a nutcracker that was "made of silver and diamonds worth $1,000." Harmond explained that he was a grown-up neighbor of mine, and invented a whole background for his character. I asked him if he'd like to join me outside for a walk with our dog, and that's when the big fun began. Instead of dropping his character, Harmond rode his bike next to me and Sampson, proudly volunteering that he was the father of five children. "My neighbor works for me," he explained. "He's a scientist. He makes bikes and supercars for me." On our way home, my son took me on a tour of his imaginary house. In reality, he was showing me a detailed sidewalk-chalk drawing he had done the day before, right in our driveway. Forgive me for bragging but I was blown away by my typically sports-focused seven-year-old—his creative mind and his ability to "stay in character" during this game he'd invented.

Gearing Up for Wet Weather

Cold rain doesn't conjure up warm images, but if you've got the right gear, you'll be warm and having fun splashing in the puddles with your kids! Children love their rain boots and raincoats. I've learned to love my cute knee-high rubber boots that I found at a discount shoe retailer and rely on a waterproof windbreaker with fleece underneath to stay dry. I'm also better now about having umbrellas handy so we can stay dry and outside longer while we walk the dog or walk to school.

And being prepared for when you come inside is even more important. One or two large rubber-lined mats are great—one for outside the door and one for inside. Wet clothes can be removed on the spot without hurting the floor and a stack of towels on hand can keep kids warm while they run up to the bath to wash off the mud!

Outdoor time stimulates my kids' imaginations. It brings out their curiosity and allows them to let off steam. This is crucial in the spring when the mild weather is yet to come and kids with pent-up energy need to be frequently motivated and redirected toward constructive activities.

I soon learned to create tools that would help me listen better to my children and act upon what interested them. Here's one example: At the beginning of every school year, I got a letter from school—a reminder to parents that we were our children's best teachers. While educated, I didn't have an education degree and I worried about my ability to know how and what to teach my children without a specific lesson and educational objectives (which, by the way, I would never commit the time to doing at home). Yes, I know, few parents are official teachers, so most of us just have to wing it. But that letter from school had me wishing for a helpful tool—a daily reminder of what I could do to foster the educational development of my children while we went about our scheduled lives.

So last spring, it finally dawned on me that simply asking questions of my children, sparking their natural curiosity, helps them to learn. And that's what inspired me to create my Rebecca Plants Curiosity Cards, fifty durable and circular cards on a portable ring, each with an open-ended question like, "What could we build with what is around us right now?" and "If you could fly like a bird, where would you go?" Questions like these not only help us learn about one another, they also lead to more questions and more interactions that help our children's brains to develop. I keep a set of Curiosity Cards by the door, one in the car, and one in my purse. My younger son likes picking the card and my older son loves reading them out loud. We've used them in restaurants, in the car, on walks, waiting in a doctor's office, or while waiting anywhere. One day, at a pick-your-own blackberry festival, we found out we'd have to wait twenty minutes for the next tractor ride. My five-year-old looked at me and asked, "Okay Mom, where are the Curiosity Cards?" We had a great conversation while we waited, which made the time fly by. (Another family played thumb war—a fabulous idea.) And after we were finished, we still had forty-nine other ideas at our fingertips.

Create Your Family's Outdoor-to-Go Kit—and Try it Out!

Be prepared for spontaneous adventures with a backpack full of what you and the kids want to have on hand:

- Picnic blanket
- Reusable water bottles
- Non-perishable snack such as pretzels
- Binoculars
- Magnifying glass
- Nature guide
- Sunscreen and bug spray
- Hand wipes
- Rebecca Plants Curiosity Cards (of course)

Keep one by the door and one in your car as a reminder to head outside for some fun. Put it together as a family and then go try it out!

march

Anticipate spring by noticing the little things.

March 21st is the official start of spring, but in many parts of the United States it still feels suspiciously like winter. Watch and listen for early signs of springtime, like tiny buds on trees and shrubs, early bulbs peeking out of the ground, and birdsong. In Virginia, the birds are becoming more active in the morning and the insects at night (according to my younger son) "sing in a symphony" long before any visual signs of spring. When the temperatures are in the forties and fifties, it's time to plant the first crop of the season: peas!

Think of the longer spring days as extra family time. Perhaps activities you once thought would only work on the weekend can now be snuck in with an extra hour of daylight. Take a walk after dinner, ride bikes, kick or catch a ball, maybe even head to the local fishing hole together. Bedtime may creep slightly later for the kids, and everyone will go to bed with smiles on their faces, thinking of the time you spent together.

March Activities

1. PICK A FAVORITE FAMILY SPOT

My sons and I often visit a footbridge over a creek about

ten minutes from our house. It's a place that we go back to again and again all year, and each time we go, we see something new and appreciate the subtle changes each season brings. Visit a favorite location with your children; better yet, if you don't have a favorite, take a walk near home and discover one.

2. SEARCH FOR THE SIGNS OF SPRING

See how many you can find. What do you hear? Look at the details around you. Talk about what looks different compared to what you last remember, and what you think will be different a month from now. What are you looking forward to doing in the months ahead? Which of those activities can you actually do now too? Try one of them!

3. MAKE A BIRD FEEDER

Make a bagel bird feeder and hang it on a tree outside within view of where you eat breakfast. All you need is a plain bagel. Cut it in half and tie a piece of twine around each half. Spread vegetable shortening or peanut butter on it, and dip it in bird seed. No bird seed? I showed twenty-six kindergartners how to sprinkle chopped raisins, apples, sunflower seeds, and corn meal onto the shortening. Using the twine (remember to tie it around the bagels before you dip them—saves a mess later), the class hung the bagel bird feeders in the school garden. The five-year-olds loved this project! No bagel? Use a pinecone instead.

4. SEE WHAT COMES OUT AT NIGHT

In the Eastern United States and Canada, the spotted sala-
mander is an amphibian that only emerges from its underground home on one rainy night in the spring to breed. What
comes out at night where you live: opossums, raccoons, owls?
Visit a local nature center or do an Internet search to learn
the signs of where the local animals may live, then look for
these signs on your nature walks. For example, salamanders
like moist environments under logs near water. Bats come
out where I live starting in March, and I've seen raccoon
prints in the mud.

5. VISIT A GARDEN

I love to visit the U.S. Botanic Garden in March in Washington,
D.C. Why visit a garden when it might still feel like winter?
Seeing an established garden just before everything bursts
in spring is a great way to find trees and shrubs and maybe
even some perennials that have great early spring interest
when you're longing for beauty outside: red chokeberry and
winterberry holly have beautiful red berries, longleaf pine
has bright green needles, star magnolia has early blooms,
and heather and hellebores also have flowers.

Think of the Outdoors as Your Personal Retreat

We can't always go on vacation, but we can always
appreciate the fresh air in the outdoor space that is
around us. Outside time can be your special time

together as a family, and your personal retreat when you need some time to yourself. You can find lots of ways to enjoy a moment: swing before school, walk at lunch, skip through the park on the way home, or observe the night sky as your planetarium. Even a bike ride on a Saturday morning and a roasted s'more in the afternoon can make a day special.

6. MAKE MUD PRINTS

Kids always seem to find the mud, so when we head outside in wintertime, even if there is no snow on the ground, I get my kids to wear their boots. Before they had boots we designated an old pair of shoes for each kid to be their "mud shoes." I don't worry about their boots or mud shoes getting muddy since they are mud-approved by Mom. Give your kids license for what you feel comfortable with: mud shoe prints, mud bike tire prints, mud handprints, no rules? Assuming we don't have to be anywhere immediately, I let my kids loose and have towels ready by the door for muddy shoes and clothes and as soon as we are home, I send the kids up to the bath ASAP!

7. RACE FOR A BALL

A guest on my radio show, *Get Out of the House*, suggested this activity. Throw the ball over your house and see who can run around the side to reach it first. If you have an apartment or your house is too tall, take the ball to the park and throw it over a tree, park bench, or tennis court net. The point is to get some exercise and laugh a lot by seeing who can get the ball first.

8. MAKE AN ADVENTURE BOOK

Introduce this notebook, inspired by the movie *Up*, while you are sitting together outside, and prompt your kids to help you think of a special place to keep it. Draw or cut out and paste pictures of places that you want to go together as a family. In our house, we have a corkboard where we paste photos of and articles about the places we want to go.

9. PLAY KICK THE CAN

In this team game of hide-and-seek, you try to stay hidden to avoid being seen by whoever is "it" and sent to jail. Your teammates can try to kick the can (an empty soda can will do) and release you from jail by calling your name, but watch out; whoever is "it" is protecting the can. If you are seen first, you are "it" for the next game. Set some rules before the game begins and make sure your kids know them: limit the area where they are allowed to hide and go over the code word(s) for when they come out. "Olly olly oxen free" is what was originally shouted to signal the end of the game and the time to come out of hiding.

10. SPROUT GRASS IN A PLASTIC CUP

Schools do this growing activity in spring, and I love it for home too. Put an inch of soil in a clear plastic cup, then sprinkle a thin layer of grass seed on the soil and sprinkle another thin layer of soil on top of the seed. Keep the soil moist and place the cup on a sunny windowsill. No drainage is needed because the grass seed needs to stay moist to grow. Over two to three weeks, you'll watch the grass seeds sprout!

11. ROLL DOWN A HILL

My kids are huge fans of rolling down hills, and the best part is that it's free and can be done anytime, anywhere. You don't even need a big hill; a small incline will do. I am not crazy about being dizzy, but I'll try at least once any productive activity my kids are laughing and giggling about over and over. Sometimes these roll-fests turn into a big group hug on the ground and we roll over and over and over, together. Just get up quickly when you reach the bottom to make sure no one gets squished!

12. GET INSPIRED WITH A FESTIVAL OR MUSEUM

You don't need an outdoor festival to have a good time, but sometimes it helps to look them up when the weather isn't inspiring you to get out on your own. No festivals? Check out local children's, natural history, or science museums. Sometimes just looking up their programs for children can kick-start a great idea of something your family can do together. For example, a museum may feature a live outdoor performance. Task the kids with putting on their own outdoor talent show for the family.

Build a Raised Vegetable Bed

Whether you build a small square (2'× 2') or a large rectangle (3'× 8'), creating a wooden frame in your yard for growing vegetables on top of the ground affords you more space than a container to grow multiple vegetables at once. March is the perfect time to put in your raised vegetable bed. Don't want a wooden frame? Mix the ground soil directly with compost and mound the soil for better drainage. For me, a 6" tall wooden frame on top of the ground makes it possible for me to work with better soil and drainage than I would otherwise have in the ground. If you don't have the space or don't want to plant vegetables in the ground, don't worry—planting vegetables in plastic pots with a diameter of 12" or greater works extremely well too.

1. Select where you would like to have your raised vegetable bed to determine the size you want. Remember, for abundant veggies, the location should get at least six hours of sun every day.
2. At the hardware store, purchase a 2"× 6" untreated board of wood, such as pine. Have the store cut the board to the length you'd like for your square or rectangle.
3. Purchase galvanized nails (which won't rust outside) as well as soil for vegetable gardening. (If you have compost at home, you can use that instead.)
4. Hammer together your boards so that your wooden frame will be 6" deep. With adult supervision, your kids can help you hammer.
5. Lay your raised vegetable frame on the ground

where you intend to keep it. Fill the frame with soil. You're ready to garden!

Consider having the raised vegetable bed belong to your children. Let them dig, plant, and water daily. They will take pride in their garden, taste their vegetables, and you can learn together!

13. LOOK FOR HAWKS

Red-tailed hawks mate in March and April and usually make their nests in the tallest trees, and they might even take over a nest that a great horned owl used in January and February. I learned this tip from David Mizejewski, naturalist with the National Wildlife Federation. And sure enough, for several days in March I heard loud and unusual birdcalls. When I looked up, there were hawks locking talons in flight. Find out from your local nature center when to look for hawks.

14. PLAY BALL FREEZE TAG

Whoever is "it" has a soft bouncy ball and chases the others. The goal is to tag someone with the ball in order to "freeze" them. A third player can try to touch their teammate to "unfreeze" them and keep the game going. My husband recently played with our sons and their friends in the yard. The kids had a blast, and needless to say, my husband got his workout for the day!

15. QUIZ ME OUTSIDE

When your kids are old enough for tests (it starts in kinder-garten!) or even if they are not, enjoy a game of learning while you are on a bike ride or walking outside. Sing your *ABC*s, do some math ("What's 2+2?"), or try a practice spelling test. Spot one, two, then three of something, or find objects in nature that start with *A*, *B*, or *C*! The fresh air and movement will make you forget that you're doing work and turn the lessons into effortless fun.

16. PLANT PEAS

When St. Patrick's Day arrives, if your temperatures are in the forties and fifties, it's the perfect time to plant sugar snap peas. Buy your pea seeds from a local nursery or catalog. Pick a sunny area in your yard or garden and prepare your soil by mixing in some store-bought organic gardening soil or compost (it's never too late to start a compost pile, but it will likely take at least three months to produce usable com-post). Use your trowel or hand shovel to drag a line an inch deep in the soil. Place peas an inch and a half apart. Keep the soil moist. Depending on where you live, you may have enough rain that you don't need to water. Seedlings will ap-pear in about two to three weeks. As the pea plants grow, put long sticks in the ground (any kind of stake or trellis) so they can vine up. You can harvest in about six to eight weeks. My boys love to visit the garden and "taste test" the peas to see if they are ready—just as I did when I was a child. Most of the peas are eaten before they make it to the dinner table! If you don't have a yard you can still plant peas in a container (with drainage holes and a saucer to catch the water) and keep it in the sun on your balcony or front stoop. Just make sure to place a stake or two (long sticks will do) for the pea plants to climb up. Whether planted in the ground or in a container, remember to water your peas daily if it hasn't rained.

17. CHECK OUT MOTHER NATURE'S COMPOST

I finally understood composting when I noticed dark, rich, black soil underneath the leaf remnants on the forest floor. The sunshine, weight and moisture from snow, and worm activity had reduced a huge layer of fallen leaves over six months to fertile ground. Seeing this firsthand will help your children relate having a compost pile at home to what happens in nature every year.

Start Your Own Compost Pile

I love having compost because it provides all the nutrient-rich soil I need for my vegetable garden. The compost bin is in the sun near my two raised vegetable beds, and my five-year-old can dig soil out of it into a bucket that he then dumps into and spreads over the beds himself with a rake. Day to day, we keep a small decorative pail with a handle on the kitchen counter where we put vegetable scraps, which are then emptied into the compost bin (a great tip from my yoga instructor, Peg Mulqueen).

It can take three to six months for a compost pile to decompose and produce soil (a lesson in patience for the whole family). Once I got through the initial six months it took for my first compost (started in winter from a compost bin I received for Christmas), I was fascinated how in the warmer months, with a compost pile comprised of chopped vegetable kitchen scraps, coffee grounds, dry leaves, plant and grass clippings, and leftover water from drinks (turned or mixed once a month), worms found their way into my compost and the process quickened to three months. There are many ways to create compost (a small pile in your yard, a bin, a large exposed pile or "lazy heap," or worm composting inside); my guess is that they all have their pros and cons. See more about methods at www.composting 101.com. The way you choose may depend on your tolerance for a natural trash heap in your environment!

18. LOOK FOR SEEDLINGS

I love noticing how nature changes, and that includes finding seedlings of new trees once the snow has melted. Tiny evergreen seedlings may be the easiest to notice first (look under the tallest trees and in a sunny spot). Then you can find new pine cones that have fallen to the ground. Mention to your kids that trees create cones or seed pods to release new seeds in hope of them taking root.

19. PLANT LETTUCE

Many varieties of greens—mesclun, romaine, arugula, kale, collards—love daytime temperatures around sixty degrees Fahrenheit. Lettuce is easy to grow in a container or raised vegetable bed—simply sprinkle the seeds and cover with a half inch of soil. Keep in the sun and water daily. My five-year-old loves showing his friends his crop of lettuce and getting them to try it. He won't eat salad inside, but he'll eat it from the garden! Plant new seeds every few days for a continuous harvest.

How to Keep the Deer and Bunnies Away

Deer and rabbits leave everything alone in my yard except my vegetable garden. So, I put up six-foot landscape stakes around the perimeter of the vegetable garden and wrap bird netting around the stakes, which keeps them out.

20. CREATE YOUR OWN POND SKIMMING

When the snow is melting on the slopes, many resorts have a tradition of "pond skimming." The staff creates a small pond of water at the bottom of a slope and skiers try to make it across. You don't have to be near a ski slope to feel a part of this seasonal fun. If you don't have snow, make a small ramp with your slip 'n' slide over a baby pool full of water and see what lightweight items will skim across: a plastic sled, a boogie board, a ball? If you have snow, create a small pool of water at the end of an incline and do the same!

21. GO FISHING OR WATCH SOMEONE FISH

The fish are biting all year; grab your fishing pole or borrow one from a friend and take the kids to a local dock. The first time I saw fishing, I was simply exploring a new park with my kids and we watched a mom who was teaching her four-year-old son and six-year-old daughter how to fish. She used pliers to attach the bait to the hook and work gloves to hold the fish when they caught one. Then she used the pliers again to remove the hook from the fish's mouth. I've learned to love artificial lures so I don't have to deal with worms, but the kids do love digging up worms and they work really well for catching fish!

22. SUPPORT YOUR LOCAL FARMERS AND LEARN

Experience the produce of the seasons and learn what is planted and when it is harvested where you live. Visit a farmer's market and show your children different types of locally grown fruits and vegetables. While you're there, ask about local farms that offer pick-your-own experiences throughout the growing season and get a calendar so you can plan ahead for the year. Can't fit in a farmer's market? Join a CSA, or Community Shared Agriculture group, where you pay a fee in exchange for locally grown, freshly harvested produce.

23. PLAY FRISBEE OR FRISBEE GOLF

My younger son is a fantastic Frisbee thrower. Me? Not so much. But we have found that the Aerobie brand of Frisbees is user-friendly for people like me, who are Frisbee-challenged. If you have fun practicing in the yard or playground, you may enjoy a local park's Frisbee golf course or you can make a course in the yard. Create five or more stations that serve as targets or "holes" for your Frisbee. For example, you could use a bucket, a Hula-Hoop, a chair, steps, and the corner of the yard. See how many throws of the Frisbee it takes to reach each hole.

24. MAKE SOMETHING FROM NATURE

My friend Starla used to make bows and arrows as a child with tiny sticks and blades of grass. What can you and your child envision and create? Make up a story that goes along with your creation. You can even write words in leaves and sticks on the ground. For example, a simple "hello" created by my son and one of his cousins was a great way to pass the time, and it was quite beautiful!

25. EXPRESS YOURSELF WITH SIDEWALK CHALK

I have a box of sidewalk chalk on a shelf of outdoor toys in the garage that the kids can pull out anytime. Sidewalk chalk is immediate fun and can be an opportunity for individual or group expression. For example, use sidewalk chalk for a tribute to each family member. Draw pictures and write words to express why you think they are great. At the end, you'll have a wonderful visual celebration of your family.

26. RACE TO SPOT THE MOST CRITTERS

Give yourselves one to five minutes to spot wildlife or insects. Just shout out what you see. This game can be played anywhere, whether in the big city, a park, car, or yard. See who notices the most, and then play again.

27. COMPARE YOUR SHADOWS

We have fun with this when the kids have friends over. First, lie on the sidewalk or driveway and have someone trace the outline of your body. Then, stand up and have someone trace your shadow. See which outline is bigger and by how much. You can even measure the difference.

28. READ GARDEN-INSPIRED BOOKS

Gear up for the planting season! Grab a blanket and head outside to read a favorite story about a garden. My favorites are "The Garden" (a short story in *Frog and Toad Together*), *The Carrot Seed*, *To Be Like the Sun*, *The Secret Garden*, and *Caillou In The Garden*.

29. FLY A KITE

In Washington, D.C., I love the Cherry Blossom Kite Festival. The sky is full of colorful kites blowing in the wind. The puffy, light pink blossoms are on the cherry trees but the green leaves on surrounding trees have yet to burst. You don't need cherry blossoms near you to fly your own kite though! Any day with wind is a great time for a kite; grab one and head outside together. With two people and a little patience, you'll be having fun!

30. WATCH THE SUNSET AS A FAMILY

Once we "spring forward" with the clocks and before the leaves burst forth from the trees, notice where you might be able to go as a family after dinner to watch the sunset. If your family is up for it, go ahead and have a picnic dinner outside. If it feels too cold for a sit-down meal, try a variation that keeps the kids more active; take a picnic blanket and your favorite family game and soak in that extra hour of daylight, together.

31. CAPTURE THE FEELING OF SPRING

Roast some s'mores as a way to celebrate the end of winter, and ask one another what you like best about being together. Feel the warmth of spring in your family's answers and all the promise it holds for some family time every day outside in the coming months.

april

Let the changing weather inspire new activities.

Depending on where you live, there may still be snow on the ground and bare trees overhead. But trust me—spring is all around you. The natural world is waking up, and the changing weather provides exciting opportunities for outside activities.

One spring morning, as we walked the dog before school, my kids discovered that our local creek was overflowing with rushing water, thanks to the previous evening's rain. They ran to pick up fallen twigs and yelled gleefully, "Pooh Sticks!" This game, played by Winnie the Pooh in A. A. Milne's *The House at Pooh Corner*, involves racing sticks in a stream, and I played it with my parents as a little girl. Thanks to their grandparents, my boys learned the game too.

That magical April day was Pooh Stick heaven. We had one race after another, each of us dropping our stick of choice on the count of three from one side of the bridge and racing over to the other side to see whose stick would come through first. At the end of each race, the boys would shout, "Let's play again!" Each time, we'd try a different size stick or wood chip to see which produced the most success.

We all were having so much fun; the simplicity and joy of the moment was inspiring.

That night, when I asked each of the boys for three great things that had happened that day, the first for each of them was Pooh Sticks. So the next time it is raining, head for a nearby creek and have some Pooh Stick fun. Even if you're by yourself, you can pick up two sticks and give it a go.

April Activities

1. CREATE A NATURE MANDALA

CreativelyFit.com founder Whitney Ferré recommends exercising our right brains for more creativity with a *mandala* or circular pattern made from any objects you find outside. Start your design from the center and spiral out with whatever pattern and objects interest you: leaves, pebbles, flowers—anything! If you find you love creating mandalas, you and your kids can also draw them over and over on the go by having a KleenSlate dry erase paddle at the ready in your bag (www.KleenSlate.com).

2. PLANT A GARDEN

April is prime planting season: the temperatures are finally milder and it's exciting to be outside, digging in the soil with your kids. If you have a yard, start a perennial garden. If you have a balcony, a stoop, a kid-safe rooftop, or even a sunny windowsill, go ahead and buy some plants with the kids and make a lovely container garden. Containers are great for growing vegetables and herbs too. Sprinkle lettuce seeds (e.g., mesclun mix) on top of soil in a container, cover with a half inch of soil, water daily in the sun, and in two to three weeks you'll have salad for your dinner! If you start herb seeds inside on a sunny windowsill, in a month you'll have seedlings for a Mother's Day gift!

3. DO SOME SPRING CLEANING

Check your shelves and closets and even the garage for toys and clothing that the kids have outgrown. You can get rid of these items with a fun outdoor yard or stoop sale, and the kids can help by making price tags and greeting neighbors who stop by, enjoying the sunshine and fresh air. They may even want to make a lemonade stand! Anything that doesn't sell can be donated to a charitable organization.

How to Plant Vegetables in Containers

Growing vegetables in containers is easy! You can keep them where you have the most sun and you don't even need a yard. My favorite vegetables for containers are peas, lettuce, tomatoes, carrots, and bell peppers.

1. For seeds, such as carrots or lettuce, choose a plastic container about the size of a 12" diameter bucket. Ensure it has drainage holes at the bottom and a saucer underneath to catch the excess water.
2. Use potting mix or half potting mix mixed with half organic gardening soil or compost.
3. Scatter the seeds on the top of the soil. Cover with less than an inch of soil and water thoroughly until the water comes out of the drainage holes

at the bottom (with a saucer underneath to catch excess water).

4. Place in a spot that gets sun all day or move the container as the sun moves to give your veggies adequate sunlight.

5. Water your container, as above, every day. This is a great activity for kids!

6. When the tiny seedlings start to appear, pinch out or remove every other seedling (or two) to create more room for each plant to grow. Discard removed seedlings in the compost or eat these "baby greens" in your salad!

7. With bell pepper or tomatoes, buy pregrown plants or seedlings or sprout pepper and tomato seeds indoors on your windowsill. In this case, plant one plant per container, and your plant will need support as it grows (so the heavy vegetables don't weigh the plant down).

8. You'll want to wait to put bell pepper, tomato, and tender herbs outside until nighttime temperatures are at least fifty-five degrees Fahrenheit.

4. SHIPS AHOY! SAIL JUICE BOX BOATS IN PUDDLES

After your kids finish their juice boxes, find a puddle and float them like boats. Make up a story about their adventures. Once the children are done playing, they can write or draw a story about their adventure and tell you about it. What a great way to encourage their creativity!

5. OUTDOOR ART FUN! CREATE FOOD COLORING WATERCOLORS

Set up your art studio outside and be inspired by nature; you don't even need paint. Food coloring and water makes watercolors. Freeze leftover paint in cups for another day. This great idea is from my friend Eli in Los Angeles, California. She always has homemade watercolors on hand for her three-year old, who loves to go out on their apartment balcony and paint the sunset.

6. MAKE A PERENNIAL GARDEN

Select a patch of ground, for example, that's four by six feet. Remove the grass and weeds and mix the soil to loosen it. Take your kids to the garden center and select six plants together. If you go after dinner there will be fewer customers, which means more help from the salespeople. Tell them whether your new garden bed is in full sun, partial sun, or shade, and ask for the most fail-proof, longest-blooming perennials. I like catmint (nepeta) and salvia—butterfly-attracting, deer-resistant staples for full and partial sun in a spring and summer garden. Buy two bags of compost and two bags of mulch. Back home, let your children help you mix the compost into your soil. When the plants are in, place mulch in between the plants on top of the soil and water daily for a week; then cut back to every other day, then every three days, etc., until you are watering once a week (or more, during dry spells).

Want to know more? My Bloom Calendar shows you

pictures of my favorite perennials, the conditions they require, and how long each blooms (www.rebeccaplants.com).

7. BOUNCE IT! ONE BALL THREE WAYS

Use one bouncy ball to play four square, then bocce ball, then bowling. For four square, draw in chalk a grid of four squares; players stand in a square and bounce the ball to each other. For bocce ball, use an object as a target and see who can roll the ball the closest to it. For bowling, set out tall plastic cups or recycled water bottles and try to knock them over.

8. FIND A SCENIC VIEW

My boys and I have a favorite mound of dirt that we visit often. One day, they climbed up and called to me, "Mom, you *have* to come see this view!" I reluctantly climbed to the top and looked. To be honest, it was pretty cool. We weren't that high up, but we had a completely different visual perspective of our neighborhood. Climb to the top of something together: a slide, hill, or dirt mound, and notice how things look different.

Pocket Nature Guides

I love my laminated pocket nature guides, for example the series from www.PocketNaturalist.com. Likely found in any local bookstore, they are specific to my state and have wonderful labeled pictures. I often keep them in the car for the kids to look at while we're driving around. The boys love to point out and talk about what wildlife they've seen before and often recount tales of when we've seen wildlife together. If we forget to put the guides in a backpack for a walk, we often look forward to taking a look at them when we return home to spot the picture of what we saw and look for its name.

9. FIND A STICK FOR A LONG JUMP

We've all heard of using walking sticks for stability on hikes, but what about a walking stick to help you jump farther? My five-year-old loves to find suitable walking sticks on the ground and uses them as a support so he can jump farther in the grass. Try it!

10. MAKE A WISH

As soon as kids can walk, they love to blow the fluffy tops of dandelions that have gone to seed. My younger son loves to seize the opportunity to blow the seeds from the flower and make a wish. Sometimes, if I'm lucky, he'll present the dandelion he picked and let me make the wish. Or we have fun trying to use our combined forces to make all the seeds float away at once.

11. SAVOR A FLOWERING TREE

Some trees flower before the leaves appear: pear, cherry, plum, redbud, dogwood. Find some flowering trees where you live. Note your favorites. You may decide you want to have those early blossoms in your yard. But more important-ly, savor the beauty of those flowering trees. Take pictures of you and your family in front of them; have picnics under them. With roughly a two- to three-week flowering span, the blooms will soon be gone. When the flower petals do fall in the wind, dance under them and enjoy a beautiful shower of petals.

12. SPLASH! RATE YOUR PUDDLE JUMP

Once the family is suited up in rain gear, head out to the puddles and start jumping! You can rate your jumps like they do in the Olympics! The biggest splash, of course, is "a perfect ten." But everyone will need to try many times to perfect their individual technique. And you'll want to splash in as many puddles as possible, since the wave effect may be different depending on how deep or long the puddle.

13. CREATE A FORT! BUILD A BEAN TEPEE

This great activity from garden designer and writer Starla J. King was one of my favorite episodes of my TV show, *Get Out of the House.* Plant seeds and watch the bean vines grow through summer, creating the perfect hiding spot and a vegetable you can harvest for meals. Pick a spot that gets at least six hours of sun a day. Find five fallen tree branches or purchase six-foot wooden stakes and twine or string. To secure the stakes for your tepee, place them three to four inches in the ground. Mix new topsoil or compost around each stake to prepare for the beans. At the top where the stakes meet, use a rubber mallet to drive each stake further into the ground, then run the twine in between and around the top of the stakes and tie it with a knot. Plant a variety of "pole" beans (versus bush) that vine, such as Kentucky Wonder. Poke three to four beans around each stake, about one inch into the soil and cover with dirt. Water once a day (kids love this). It's fun to check on growth every day. Sprouts will appear in one to two weeks.

14. NOTICE THE UNDERSTORY

When we think of spring, sometimes it seems that we go from "no leaves" to "green leaves everywhere" overnight. But really the transition to a full flush of leaves is much more gradual. Find a patch of woods and look closely at the buds on each of the trees. Then step back and take a look at all the trees. Typically, there is a layer of trees in the understory (underneath the taller trees) that starts to "leaf out" first, showing an ethereal dusting of bright green between the shortest and the tallest trees. Observe the trees over several days and see if you can notice daily changes. Have the kids document this process with drawings or photographs.

15. ROTATE SNACK TIME OUTSIDE

Sometimes it's helpful to have a part of my kids' routine take place outside, like snack time. I keep a picnic blanket by the door, and often I will proactively set up the blanket with snacks and let them know it is there to avoid any opportunity for protest. Usually, the kids will happily go to wherever I set up the food and drink. Rotate the spot around the house and have them find it. Put their backpacks or books there too and homework or reading outside can follow. No yard? Take your Outdoor-To-Go Kit and head together to your favorite nearby snack spot.

16. CLUES EVERYWHERE! WATCH THE BIRDS

In April, birds offer many clues about what is happening all around us. Act as a scientist and start to observe and record the changes happening with the birds. Are they building nests? How are the birds interacting? When do they make the most sound—morning, afternoon, or evening? Which birds do you see most often, and what do they look like? Back at home, look up more information about the birds you've seen, based on their colors and markings and behavior. Here is a website to get you started: www.AllAboutBirds.org.

17. DIG IN! GIVE YOUR CHILD A PLACE TO DIG

Even with their own garden, many kids want to dig over and over just for the sake of exploring. Consider setting aside a 2'x2' square area of dirt just for digging. You can keep any tools and accessories for the digging spot in a small basket or bucket by the door: hand shovel, gloves, and magnifying glass. Your child can return the basket to the same spot so they can find their tools next time. ·

18. FOLLOW THE WATER

In the rain, it's interesting to see where the water goes. Follow it together. It may flow down a street and into a storm drain or, better yet, you may know of a nearby creek. Search upstream to find where the water starts to flow toward the creek. One rainy afternoon, my boys and I found a clear pond with lots of frogs that forked into two narrow meandering paths of water, which then flowed into a creek. We even came across a turtle enjoying the wet weather.

19. SEE YOUR REFLECTION

Puddles are great for noticing your reflection, and if you tap the water gently, you'll see how the ripples impact the way your reflection looks. Even more interesting is noticing your reflection in tiny droplets of water dangling from tree branches and leaves. The convex shape of the droplet stretches your reflection. What else do you see while looking in the reflection of a rain drop?

Eat Outside!

Do you dream of dining al fresco? Why not enjoy eating outside more often? It's as easy as a picnic blanket or using that patio furniture that is sitting outside your door. In the morning, have your cup of coffee or breakfast outside. Have an aperitif before dinner as the French do, with a snack and juice for the kids and a glass of wine or sparkling water for you. Sandwiches can even be brought to sports practices. As the weather changes, you can accommodate the changes too: an umbrella over the table in the rain, a fan for a breeze in warm weather, a citronella candle for mosquitoes. (My cousin Martine in Luxembourg uses a regular candle sprayed with a little citronella oil—brilliant!)

20. LOOK FOR TADPOLES

Find a pond and visit it often. What do you see? Do you see tadpoles? In the spring, frogs call loudly at night, searching for their mates. Just two to three days later, tiny black specks appear in the water that miraculously grow into tadpoles in approximately six days. Over several weeks, tiny frogs will develop and make their way on to land, living in and around water.

21. CROSS A CREEK OR LOG TOGETHER

There is something adventurous about crossing a natural bridge, whether it's made from rocks in shallow water or a fallen log. Help one another cross by holding hands. Parents or an older sibling may want to try crossing alone first, to make sure the rocks or log are stable and not too slippery, before helping little ones across.

22. PLANT FOR EARTH DAY, ARBOR DAY, AND KEEP AMERICA BEAUTIFUL WEEK

The third and fourth weeks in April provide lots of opportunities to think about our connection to the Earth. Planting is a great way for kids to experience firsthand how the Earth gives back to us. Have two or more projects, at least one for your family and one for your community, such as your local school. Plant a vegetable such as peas or beans or plant a tree seedling in someone's memory or for shade on the school playground. Have the kids tell you what they have learned in school about taking care of the Earth and conserving resources.

23. DISCOVER A NATURAL OBSTACLE COURSE

This activity takes crossing a creek or log one step further. Invite your children to observe the natural landscape and design a path or route to explore. For example, your child might decide to climb over a log, creep under a tree, race to the third tree and back, and then touch the rock and you're done. Then you're ready to design more paths, and can discuss after you try them all which you like best and why.

24. LOOK AT MOSS AND MUSHROOMS

Moist spring conditions create vibrant green moss and interesting fungi. We love noticing what is popping up along forest paths and in the yard. We like touching fuzzy moss too. The site www.Backyardnature.net has some interesting general information about moss and mushroom identification.

25. DETERMINE FROM WHICH TREE THE BRANCH FELL

As the leaves fill the trees, it may not be as obvious that there are large sections or large branches that have fallen from trees. As you walk, notice fallen branches; see if your child (perhaps with your help) can find which tree a specific branch fell from by looking above for the broken tree limb.

26. COMPARE ROCKS

Children love to dig up rocks. Do they all look the same? How is their texture similar? Go to a patch of dirt down the street and dig up some more rocks. How are those different? If you don't know the topography and geological history of where you live, a series of questions on www.RockHounds.com/rockshop/rockkey can tell you what types of rocks you may be finding underground or about the boulders laying on top of the ground in your neighborhood.

27. PLAY FOLLOW THE LEADER

One of my best memories of my husband with the kids was in a local park. The kids were out of things to do and he suddenly said, "Follow me." It was almost a version of Simon Says where his quick decisions were designed to see if the kids were paying attention. The kids had to follow behind him and do everything he did, from running and then suddenly stopping, to circling trees three times and crawling under picnic benches, to flapping their arms. He changed his movements so many times that they never bored of it, and the sight had me in stitches.

28. STOP BY THE PARK ON YOUR WAY HOME

Another routine to get out of the house that's easy to re-member is to stop by the park on your way home with the kids. Bring a snack along or pick up sandwiches before-hand for a picnic dinner. Keep a picnic blanket in your car and you'll have everything you need for dinner, play, and homework outside until the sun goes down.

29. WRITE YOUR *ABC*S WITH STICKS

Gather sticks and make letters, words, or special messages such as "I love you." If your kids are spelling, you can even play a version of Hangman where sticks represent the spaces for letters in a word. Fill in correctly guessed letters with sticks or use chalk instead.

30. CLIMB A "MOUNTAIN"

Sometimes a routine path can get boring; find a nearby hill to walk up for an adventure and some exercise. The size of the hill you need depends on the size of your child. The smaller the child, the smaller the hill! Walk up, down, and around. Remember to take a bottle of water with you and maybe even a snack to eat as you chat and rest at the top.

may

As the weather improves, try bigger adventures!

Major holidays offer great opportunities for outdoor adventure. One year, when Mother's Day rolled around, I proposed a family walk in Virginia's Shenandoah National Park. I made it more special by inviting my parents to join us. Our one-hour hike, taken from a book called *Easy Day Hikes in Shenandoah National Park*, turned into a highly enjoyable (if at times strenuous) three-hour trek—not because we got lost, but because we were having a blast and decided to track down a waterfall we'd spotted on the trail map.

My parents are in their sixties and in decent health, but they're not regular hikers. My father has Lyme disease from a deer tick that landed in his sock in Arlington, Virginia, ten years ago. His energy fluctuates and he has chronic issues with pain. Whenever he's around his grandchildren his spirits lift, but I didn't know if he'd have the energy for the hike, not to mention the hour-long drive each way. Still, they accepted the invitation with enthusiasm and I knew we could tailor the outing to everyone's pace.

When we arrived at the national park, it was inspiring to see other families from all walks of life celebrating

Mother's Day in a similar fashion. We had a picnic lunch on top of a mountain at the southern end of the park and then set off on our expedition. Our walking pace was comfortable; we stopped whenever anyone wanted to look at something along the way, examining twisted tree roots, countless ferns, wild geraniums with delicate purple flowers, and mossy cliffs with water gently dripping down.

That's when we started to hear the sound of rushing water.

Following the sound, we found a wide stream with water tumbling over the rocks. We were at our turnaround point but the urge to find out where that water was going was just too strong. Everyone agreed: let's keep going!

We ambled through an emerald-green, shady forest, held hands to cross a small creek, then traveled down another steep path. After walking for an hour and a half, we found an amazing overlook. We were not even halfway down the mountain but now we could see the top of a beautiful waterfall below us, in the distance.

Satisfied with our team effort, we headed back up the mountain. My husband and the boys played a made-up game called "rocks and roots," where you could only step on rocks or tree roots to climb the steep path. My mother and I fell behind the others, using my laminated guide to the flowers of Virginia to identify some of the blooms we were passing. Knowing my father, husband, and boys were together, we took our time. We chatted with some other hikers who pointed out a beautiful jack-in-the-pulpit, a green and purple striped flower that looks like a long cup hidden under its leaves. When we heard birdcalls, we got out the binoculars and a picture guide to the birds of Virginia. Sharing this rare one-on-one time with my mom in such gorgeous surroundings was a rare treat.

Mom and I met up with "the boys" half an hour after they had arrived at the end of the trail, and we congratulated everyone—ages five to sixty-two—on their stamina and all-around good spirits. Heading home, we took the Skyline Drive, a scenic route that gave us beautiful views of the Blue Ridge Mountains. Along the way, we stopped to watch our first black bear grazing on the side of a mountain. What a thrilling day. While my chosen activity started as a hike, it ended with so much more than I anticipated: newfound energy from my ill father, special moments with my mother, and a memory for my children that will last a lifetime.

Whether you have this same experience—or want to—is not as important as deciding how you and your family want to spend your time outside together. For me, it was a good reminder that while spring is a great time for short expeditions, it's also time to think about bigger adventures as the weather improves. And of course for Mother's Day, the moms get to choose.

May Activities

1. THROW A PLANTING PARTY!

Whether it's for a birthday party, a service project (e.g., beautifying your school's grounds), or a family reunion, a planting party is a great way to spend meaningful time together. With help from an adult, even a toddler can hold a hand shovel and dig with you. Older kids can dig in the dirt, plant seeds, pull weeds, or snip off dead flowers, and they are happy, focused, and learning with you. Ask people to bring their shovels and gloves of all sizes, and there will be plenty of tools to go around.

Plant Great Ideas for Summer and Watch Them Grow!

In May, the summer is almost here. So if you haven't done it already, talk to your family about their hopes for the summer. Last year, my kids wanted more family time and less time at camp, and my husband and I wanted to stick closer to home, to avoid the expense of air travel. I wanted to plant my garden with the boys and watch it grow. A family garden is an outdoor landscape that gives something to everyone in your family. Whether it's a backyard space, balcony, windowsill, city roof, community park, or school garden, it's a space you can nurture throughout the year—planting, watering, weeding, and planting again—and also a space where you notice what happens as a result of your work together.

2. INVITE BIRDS INTO YOUR GARDEN

Fill a bird feeder and hang it outside where you can see it from inside the house. Inviting birds into your garden is a great way to experience the wildlife in your area and offer the birds a wonderful treat. I've always had bird feeders within view, and they make for great conversation as a family. At around this time, you may start seeing birds, such as robins, begin making their nests and attracting a mate.

3. NOTICE CHANGES IN THE WATER

Take the kids to explore your local pond or creek, or seek out big puddles after it has rained, and see if you can spot any little creatures. Throughout the year, you might find dragonflies, frogs, toads, lizards, snakes, and even herons living near the pond. My kids have become experts in the difference between frogs and toads (the toads have bumpy backs) and they love carefully picking up a frog or toad for a closer look.

4. GIVE THE DOG A BATH

Here's an example of turning a chore into a fun family activity. All you need is a portable tub, doggie shampoo, and a garden hose with a gentle setting. And a dog, of course! No dog? You can offer to give your neighbor or a relative's dog a bath, or a child's favorite bicycle works too.

5. HAVE SOME BEACH BALL FUN

Where I live, the pool isn't open until the end of May, but that doesn't mean we can't have some fun with a beach ball. My kids and I love to play our version of volleyball, counting how many times we can hit the ball back and forth to each other. Does one of you need to get out some frustration? Toss the beach ball to the other person and have them punch it. It's even more fun if you try to catch it when it heads rapidly your way.

6. TRY SOME WACKY HULA-HOOP GAMES

For two dollars, a lightweight Hula-Hoop can provide endless fun. Not only can you try to whirl it around your waist, wrist, or neck like you used to do as a kid you can also toss it to each other vertically in the air or horizontally like a Frisbee. I even use a Hula-Hoop for my version of a beanbag toss, where you try to toss your flip-flops in the circle!

7. CREATE A WATER BOTTLE JAMBOREE

Staying hydrated while you're outside is important; why not have fun with your water bottles at the same time? Of course, the water inside is to drink. Tap the outside with your fingernails, hands, or sticks for a musical jam session. Reusable water bottles come in all shapes, sizes, and materials. See how they sound different from one another and how the sound changes as you drink your water down!

8. PLAY PRESIDENT OF THE HILL

You don't need a big hill, just an incline like one you would roll down. The person at the top of the hill is the president. One or more others are at the bottom of the hill. The president kicks a ball to the others at the bottom. If someone catches the ball, the president is out and heads to the bottom of the hill and the person who caught the ball heads to the top.

9. POT FLOWERS FOR MOTHER'S DAY

Last year, for Mother's Day, I asked my kids to pick out colorful annuals for a hanging basket: a combination of trailing and non-trailing flowers. Whether you select a hanging basket on a shepherd's hook or a decorative container, just be sure there are holes for drainage at the bottom. Water every day in full sun (remember, kids LOVE to water). Add water-soluble granular fertilizer weekly in the watering can and clip blooms as they fade to keep the flowers blooming through fall! I really loved my basket filled with different colored impatiens, perfect for an area with more shade than sun, and the kids even learned how to water them for me by touching the soil and watering them every other day or when the soil started to dry.

What Mom Really Wants for Mother's Day

No matter how old your kids are, what often matters most to Mom is a meaningful experience together as a family. Here are more outdoor gift ideas that don't cost much and are at the top of Mom's list:

- *Take a scenic hike.* With a basket of wildlife guides, binoculars, a magnifying glass, and snacks, plan an easy hike at a nearby local, state, or national park. If your children are small, a one-mile loop can be a fun and easy way to get fresh air. If you don't know where to go, try the NatureFind (www.nwf.org/naturefind) to find the right park or trail for your family.
- *Prepare a picnic.* Even with a blanket in the yard, taking the time to prepare a favorite lunch with lemonade

and a bouquet of flowers shows your appreciation for all Mom does for the family every day.

- *Visit a garden.* There are wonderful local gardens open for Mother's Day and you can present this idea to Mom with some window boxes or hanging baskets with flowers that you planted for her.
- *Give Mom an adventure.* Ask Mom what she has always wanted to do outside and take her. Whether going on a biking trail or visiting a lake and renting a canoe, ask what would be most fun for her.

10. HAVE A RAIN-SOAKED ADVENTURE

Amusement park flume rides soak riders and spectators with a big splash at the end of the track. But have you ever been completely and purposefully soaked from a spring rainstorm? Once I walked to pick up the kids from school and it unexpectedly poured on us on the way home. Instead of running straight to the house (since we were wet anyway, but not cold), I suggested we continue to a nearby trail to see what we could find, and the kids excitedly led the way. When we returned home and into warm clothes, it was a nice excuse to snuggle up and read a story with an unseasonably delightful cup of hot cocoa.

11. WATCH COMPOSTING IN A CLEAR BAG

Want to try a composting experiment? Get a large closeable plastic bag, shovel in dirt with worms, poke about twenty holes near the top of the bag for ventilation, then add banana peels and apple cores as you have snacks and watch what happens over a couple of weeks. This is great to take into school for the class to see too. Keep the bag at the outdoor temperature and away from direct sunlight. Return the worms to the spot you borrowed them from when you are done with your experiment.

12. PICK WEEDS, THEN FLOWERS

One of my Curiosity Cards reads, "What is something you don't like to do, and how could you make it more fun?" I say, if you're going to pick weeds (which needs to be done on an ongoing basis, a little at a time), why not reward yourself after? My kids and I always give ourselves a goal of seeing how fast each of us can fill up a bucket with weeds. I toss all of the weeds in a separate pile from my compost in the back of the yard to bake in the sun and decompose in case some of them have already produced seeds that I don't want in my compost. Then the kids get to go around with me and help me decide which flowers to clip to bring inside for a bouquet.

13. ATTRACT BUTTERFLIES WITH PLANTS IN CONTAINERS

This is a fun planting activity that doesn't require a lot of space! Select a location that gets at least four hours of sun; think about a spot that you see from a window or sit by on a patio or porch. All you need are various sizes of containers for interest and a bag or two of potting soil, then add plants such as white and purple salvia, yarrow (which comes in many colors), and catmint. All are long-blooming perennials that come back every year. Then, just sit back and wait for the butterflies to show up.

14. CHECK ON YOUR PEAS

If you planted your peas in forty to fifty degree weather around St. Patrick's Day and kept them in the sun and watered daily when it didn't rain, then it's time to check on their growth! You'll likely notice that the pea plants have flowered and pods are starting to emerge from the flowers. It's exciting for kids to check daily and see how the pods are getting bigger; feel free to begin tasting them with each check-in. The peas will likely be teeny-tiny now, but you'll notice in a week or two that when you split the pod open, the sweet-tasting peas are bigger! Once they are kid-tested to be the sweetest, harvest all pods that size over the next few days. If the peas get too big, they'll taste tough and bitter.

15. TAKE A POPSICLE BREAK

Now is when I start having popsicles on hand as an incentive to get the kids outside after school or dinner, since my rule is outside is where the kids need to eat anything messy. When I was little, my mom would freeze juice in popsicle molds; that is still fun. But, similar to having muffin mix on hand for a warm treat outside in winter, popsicles are my have-on-hand snack for anytime above sixty degrees. And popsicles drive other neighborhood kids to stop by for a snack and outdoor playtime with my kids.

16. PLANT YOUR SUMMER VEGETABLES

By May 15th, most of the northern United States has had its last frost. Once you're done harvesting any early spring vegetables, you can use your same space and soil to plant summer vegetables that thrive in temperatures between seventy and eighty degrees. I recommend buying inexpensive seedlings (small plants) for tomatoes, bell peppers, and eggplants to plant at this time. Try summer vegetables by seed such as carrots, cucumbers, and corn. Remember to have the kids water (every day if it hasn't rained) and weed; tomatoes and peppers will need a wire cage to support the vegetables. As for watering, I suggest picking a consistent time for the kids to do it so everyone remembers—for example, before they leave the house in the morning or after they get home. A fresh layer of compost over the old soil is not a must, but it gives your seeds a good start.

Turn Your Vegetable Garden Over to Your Kids

At the end of last season, I decided that the vegetable garden wouldn't be mine; it would belong to my children. Yes, the temptation is to control it for them, to tell them that they have to plant certain things at a certain time, to make them plant in straight rows, and to not let them harvest before the "perfect" time. Nevertheless, I decided it is okay to have a grand experiment. There are no rules. I read the seed packet information to them, but the children decide what to plant and in what pattern and when. I offer advice but I leave it up to them to take it or not, like suggesting they save an empty row to plant the same seeds the next week to extend the harvest

Learn together. Check every day to see what happens. Celebrate the seedlings. Don't limit yourself to raised beds; plant in plastic containers (the easiest veggies and herbs to grow work in containers too). Have an experience as a family that lasts beyond your time outside by bringing your harvest to gatherings and sharing with neighbors. Learn to try new vegetables and laugh as you smile or make silly faces at the taste.

Want to know more? My easy-to-follow guide, Growing Vegetables: The Basics, helps show you step-by-step how to start and care for a vegetable and herb garden (www.rebeccaplants.com).

17. MAKE SPORTS EASY

I'm not very sport-inclined, but I've learned to make it easy for me to encourage my kids' interests without having to precisely match the level of skill and passion my kids possess. Baseball and softball? I ask them to use a plastic bat and a wiffle ball (or beach ball for the littlest ones). Football? Rather than running plays against my son, I'm the quarterback and we run plays together. (I throw the ball to him.) Tennis? I teach them to bounce the tennis ball lightly up and over to me, or we practice bouncing a beach ball back and forth with our rackets, which is much easier for hand-eye coordination.

18. TAKE A DAILY ROUTINE OUTSIDE ON A BLANKET

As the weather gets warmer, more of our day-to-day routine can be performed outside. I've mentioned picnics in the yard for meals and snacks. Think about using that picnic blanket for reading in the yard or homework. Another twist: a friend of mine preps whatever dinner vegetables she can outside while her three-year-old plays with her dolls beside her.

19. START PLANNING YOUR BACKYARD CAMPOUT

The National Wildlife Federation's (NWF) annual Great American Backyard Campout is the last Saturday of June. Camping in the backyard or at a local park is a great opportunity to trade in screen time for new family experiences outside. NWF filmed my moms-and-kids-only campout, and we were treated to a nature walk with NWF wildlife expert David Mizejewski during which we saw a red-tailed hawk. The NWF website (www.backyardcampout.org) offers tons of camping tips and the opportunity to register your event. Best of all, if you forget any supplies, you're close to home.

20. THANK A BAT AND A DRAGONFLY

Like bats, dragonflies eat mosquitoes. Find a nearby pond and watch for dragonflies. How many do you see? Do some look different than others? At dusk, watch overhead for bats. If your exploration makes you want to learn more about these creatures, check out these websites: www.Dragonfly-Site.com and www.Bats4Kids.org.

21. IMAGINE YOUR OWN TOWN

Here's a fun creative game that I see kids at recess playing when I work in our local school garden. Have your child imagine wherever you may be (yard, the park, visiting grandma, even waiting outside somewhere) is her town. Ask her to take you on a tour and then each of you can take on roles in the town. Bushes can turn into storefronts, sidewalks into roads, leaves and sticks into currency. It will be fun to see where your child's imagination takes you both!

22. HAVE A GARDEN OR TEA PARTY

You don't have to have a large gathering to have a garden or tea party. Any day is a day to celebrate something. Pick a day of the week and announce to the kids that you are going to have a garden or tea party together, and ask them what would make it special. What's fun about this is you get lots of different ideas, big and small. Depending on your time and level of enthusiasm, you get to decide what is possible from their brainstorm. The most important part is that you have special time together, and any ideas that you don't get to, you have in the back of your mind for the future.

23. ASK "WHAT IF WE TRIED...? WHAT WOULD WE NEED?"

There are lots of times when my kids and I are waiting around out of the house and we need a way to pass the time. Start exploring what you'd like to try as a family. For example, "What if we tried fishing? What would we need?" You don't have to know all the answers; what is helpful is the opportunity to hear about and discuss different ideas. For example, I would answer, "I need a way not to touch the worms or the fish!"

24. SHADOW DANCE

On a day when you can see your shadows, start making funny moves and watch your shadows dance. This can be very fun and funny. The more shadows dancing, the more fun and funnier it gets.

25. CONDUCT THE BIRDCALLS

Have you ever noticed that a birdcall has a cadence or a pattern? Listen for the birds, try to notice the rhythm of the birdcall and conduct it with your hands. Sometimes we even do interpretive dance to the birdcall beat (and hope no one is watching). If you were a bird, how would your birdcall sound?

26. WRITE A STORY OUTSIDE

As a parent, I want to keep track of the wonderful things my kids say, and I usually forget to do it. This activity gives you the opportunity to capture wonderful responses from your children. Take a notebook, pencil, and crayons and find a comfy place to sit outside together. Have your child answer these questions, taken from my set of fifty Curiosity Cards: "What do you like about being outside?" and "Imagine the best day of your life. What are you doing? Who is there? What makes the day so special?" Have your child (or you, for small children) write their answers and illustrate a picture to go with the story.

27. LEARN SOME HAND-CLAPPING GAMES

My father calls the rhythmic games like "patty cake" hand-clapping games, and as my three sisters and I got older, we introduced him to more and more of them. As early as four years old, my sons started learning hand-clapping games at preschool and would teach me. Show your children a game or two that you used to play as a child and who knows? Maybe they'll have one to teach you.

28. PLAY KICKBALL

I love kickball because you can get a group of different ages together, starting from just old enough to run, and the big kids can help the little ones. It's a great game for family gatherings and even the grandparents can join in the fun. We typically use whatever is handy for the three bases. Similar to baseball, one person pitches (this time rolling the ball to home plate), and a person on the other team kicks the ball, runs around the bases, and gets a point when he or she is either out or reaches home plate.

29. TAKE AN INSIDE TOY OUTSIDE

We've given lots of highly used, ready-to-be-retired toys new life by turning them into outside toys. A play kitchen, school buses, paints, plastic swords, and magic wands—all can be turned into props for imaginative play and creative outdoor art. Keep these special outdoor toys in a bin by the back door or garage so they can have a specific storage spot.

30. CHECK ON YOUR SEEDLINGS

Now is a good time to check to see if you have seedlings sprouting from where you planted seeds for summer vegetable crops. My kids love to run out to their vegetable garden daily when they get home from school to see what changes are taking place. Don't forget to remind them to water and weed their garden.

31. FIND AND WATCH SOME WORMS

A shovelful of compost is great for this game, or, if you don't have compost, pick a patch of ground where you'll let your kids dig with a small hand shovel or their hands. Then, discover as many worms as you can find. I'm not big on handling worms myself, but my kids aren't scared, so I use gloves and the kids use their hands. You may find big worms and baby worms.

summer

USE YOUR CHILDHOOD MEMORIES
OF SUMMER TO HELP YOU

When I was growing up in Arlington, Virginia, my three sisters and I had our summers free to roam in the backyard and around our neighborhood, visiting with friends and going to the pool in a nearby apartment complex. We put on plays for the neighbors and one summer we created a "circus" to raise money for muscular dystrophy. But my absolute favorite activity with my sisters was going to the pool. During the week, when my father got home from work, he would always join us for a swim. I still have happy memories of splashing around with my family.

I am grateful that my mother was able to be at home for us. But with my own full-time business to maintain, I needed to figure out how to do outdoor activities that worked within my schedule. This meant carving out playtime with my boys before taking them to day camp. Sometimes we had quick picnic breakfasts outside, and sometimes we played tag or practiced rolling down a big hill before their camping days started.

With simple changes to my routine, I ended up having the best summer of my life. For example, I'd find an hour to head to the pool or bring out the slip 'n' slide or sprinkler whenever the kids' friends came over. We had an endless supply of popsicles that enticed the neighbors to come outside and play. Every evening, we'd take a family bike ride or walk. I also took a couple of afternoons off to take my kids on nearby adventures to lakes and swimming holes that enabled us to experience new places while keeping cool.

Your "Magic" Bag

The following items are great to have waiting by the door or in the car so you are prepared to have fun anytime in the heat of summer. When I travel by car with the kids, I call it my Magic Bag, and the kids ask for it by name because they know that is where the toys are when we're away from home and they want to have some fun.

- Playing cards, Curiosity Cards, a Frisbee, bubbles, and a small bouncy ball
- A couple of pool toys, such as an inflatable beach ball and dive rings
- Ice water bottles to drink
- An easy snack, such as apples
- Hats to shade your heads

- Sunscreen and bug spray
- Swimsuits and towels; consider swim shirts with SPF for ease
- First aid kit, tissues, and/or hand wipes
- If your kids can't swim yet, Coast Guard–approved life vests

Luckily for me, my wonderful husband had arranged a series of week-long day camps for the boys that were aligned with their interests. But I wanted summer to be about more than scheduled activities, and the boys had told me that they wanted plenty of family time. Remembering my own childhood passion for the local pool, I made sure my kids got to experience the same thing. The pool we belong to is not as fancy as my childhood pool, but we enjoy it immensely. Oddly, this community pool, shared by hundreds of single-family houses, is rarely used in the summertime.

Typically, it takes us thirty minutes to ride our bikes to the pool. We take our time, sometimes stopping by the school garden to see what's in bloom. We bring a backpack for snacks, water bottles, sunscreen, and towels. At the pool, we make up games with whatever is on hand. Inflatable rings and beach balls are fun toys—not only in the water, but also in the grass, and the kids make up countless games with these toys. They play beach ball soccer in between rounds of swimming.

We also do plenty of wildlife watching. Last summer, we saw five baby sparrows hatch from a nest made of mud above the women's restroom, and we watched their parents taking turns flying from the nest to feed them. Once the birds had grown bigger, we witnessed their first flight. In June, we also watched herons flying along the same path we took when we biked to the pool. One heron even landed on a neighboring lawn and then took off again, flying right over our house. What an amazing sight!

It was such a joy to reconnect with the feeling of summer that I always relished as a kid. And you can do this too, in simple ways, every day. When you think back on those endless days of childhood, what were you doing? Would your kids enjoy those same activities? Try one little thing each day that brings back that sense of endless summer for you and your family, whether it's taking your kids on an evening walk to get a snow cone, renting a canoe and fishing, or going to a community "splash pad" or play-approved fountain where you and your kids can jump around together.

Safety in the Woods

As leaves start to sprout and the temperatures warm, poison ivy, poison oak, ticks, snakes, and bears might be in the back of your mind. I don't care to run into any of these things, and it's helpful to know how to try your best to make sure you don't (at least not uncomfortably up close).

- Look up what poison ivy and poison oak look like. If you still have trouble remembering, like I always do, stay away from plants with three shiny leaves and vines that are fuzzy.

- Familiarize yourself with whether you have deer ticks in your area and what they look like. The most important thing to remember is to check everyone in your family for ticks—head to toe—after you've been in the woods. I usually do it before we get into the house. If I do find one, I have a pair of tweezers to pick it up (I avoid doing it by hand), and I put it in a tissue and flush it down the toilet.

- For the above hazards as well as snakes and bears, stick to marked trails; making noise will likely keep them from wanting to be near you (although you may scare away another wild creature you're hoping to see).

june

"I've always wanted to…"
The weather is right for it, whatever it may be.

Big, expensive trips were off the table for my family last year, but I still had the best summer of my life. Why? Because of the many ways that I incorporated the outdoors into my daily schedule with the kids. How did I want to feel at the end of the summer? I wanted to know that I had savored every moment, something that I remembered doing when I was a kid.

Plan some fun day trips on the weekends to local parks, lakes, or other scenic areas. Include friends and family you'd like to spend more time with, and keep in mind their levels of fitness. Don't forget to pack lunch, beverages, sunscreen, bug spray, and a magnifying glass. And think about this: having family get-togethers outside means that no one has to clean up the house for company!

June is also a perfect month to focus on your garden. Whether you have a big backyard, a small container garden, or a city rooftop, you still have plenty of options for planting with your kids. Tomatoes, peppers, herbs, and annual and perennial flowers are all easy to grow and the rewards (especially the edible crops) are great.

Remember: June is National Get Outdoors Month, so it's a great time to practice an outdoor lifestyle that will take you into the rest of the summer.

June Activities

1. FIND A STRAWBERRY FESTIVAL

Our local strawberry festival is the first weekend in June; when is yours? Ask around—that's how I found out about one within twenty minutes of our home. Like a lot of produce, there is nothing quite like the taste of a strawberry picked from the vine. It's a great melt-in-your-mouth taste. You may even be inspired to plant your own strawberry crop, which you can do now if your garden centers are carrying the plants. Your plants may be in the ground for more than one season before your first crop, but it is well worth the wait.

2. GO TO AN OUTDOOR POOL IN THE EVENING

Sure, sunny weekend days at the pool are great, but work into your routine a weekday evening at the pool with the kids. Take advantage of the longer daylight and cool off after a hot day. You can even take a picnic dinner with you. The kids have an active place to get out their energy, and they'll sleep great that night!

3. DRAW THE LANES

One of my favorite memories of kindergarten was when my class rode tricycles in the gym, set up with lanes, stop signs, and stop lights; we pretended we were driving. Use chalk on the driveway or sidewalk to make a track for bicycles or scooters; work in stop signs and stop lights. Have your child help you decide where they should be, then watch their fun as they experience their road system. Maybe you'll join in the fun too!

4. PLANT AND SHADE SOME LETTUCE

I love mesclun seeds because they are ready to clip and harvest for a salad in three weeks. While lettuce generally likes sixty to seventy degree temperatures, you can keep growing lettuce into the summer if you make a little shade over it with cheesecloth tied to four sticks. Sprinkle the seeds over some soil in a container with drainage holes, cover with another sprinkling of soil, keep in the sun, and water daily. Try it and see what happens!

5. GET WET!

There are so many ways to enjoy water in the summertime. Make slip 'n' slide play dates or plan a trip to the beach or swimming lake if there's one within driving distance. Rent a rowboat or go sailing or canoeing. Host a water-play party extravaganza in your yard, or just play in the hose!

6. KEEP ENJOYING NATURE

Count with your children how many playgrounds and trails you know about. Then, start talking about how to fit them into your schedule. Do you have time to go to one every evening? Once a week? Set a goal and then start. Keep a backpack filled with full water bottles, sunscreen, towels, and bug spray in the car for these planned trips as well as spontaneous adventures.

7. HAVE A RECESS SHOW-AND-TELL

If your kids are in preschool or elementary school, many times recess is their favorite part of the day. Ask them to show you what they like to do at recess and you'll have a slew of new ways to remind your kids in summer how they have fun outside. Asking them while school is fresh in their minds gives you a helpful supply of ideas for when they say, "I'm bored!"

Keep School Lessons Alive in Summer

You can bring fun educational activities into your kids' summer routine in simple ways. For example, kids can make predictions and then track the growth of their vegetables on a calendar or in a journal: when planted, date of first sprout, first flower, first vegetable observed, and last vegetable harvested. For older kids, how did the answers differ among types of vegetables? For children really into this activity, they can also write the temperature each day and whether it rained on a calendar. Based on the weather, they can discuss how they think the weather affected the plant growth and harvest.

If your kids are interested in gardening and you don't have a plot of your own to weed and cultivate, see if your school has a garden that might need some help over the summer. Sign up to take your kids over to their school to water and weed. Caring for the space introduces them to community service and involves them in an outdoor learning space.

8. GATHER AT THE PARK

Whenever there is a gathering with kids involved, whether a play date, birthday party, dinner with friends, or even a business meeting, consider meeting up at a park. Playgrounds are always fun for the children and have plenty of space for lots of people. Ask each family to bring a blanket, snacks or sandwiches, and water. No playground at the park? No problem. Toss a ball or a couple of your child's favorite outdoor toys into a bag.

9. JUMP ROPE

Even if your kids are too young to jump rope on their own, keeping a jump rope on hand to use when there are adults helping could turn into some fun family time. There are plenty of other ways to use this toy, such as limbo, a tug of war on the grass, or wiggling the rope on the ground and pretending to jump over a snake or a wiggly worm.

10. CREATE A SACK OR RELAY RACE

Most of us don't have burlap sacks on hand (I certainly don't), so I encourage the kids to make up variations of group races in the grass. Hop to a finish line, walk backward, walk like a crab on all fours (bottom up and feet first), or have a relay run around a large circle and pass off a rolled up piece of paper to the next runner in place of a baton. You will likely get asked to participate; please say yes! We adults can use the exercise too.

11. GIVE A BACKYARD OR GARDEN TOUR

Ask your child to show a friend or a neighbor what you've planted together! Every time I suggest this to my five-year-old, he proudly takes his friends to his 3' × 8' raised vegetable garden. After one recent tour, our four-year-old neighbor ran back to his parents, shouting with excitement, "Mom, Warner has lettuce!" My son always offers an off-the-vine taste of whatever is ripe and most kids happily participate. If you don't have a garden, don't worry— your child can still share with your guest the wonders of your backyard.

12. CELEBRATE NATIONAL GET OUTDOORS DAY

National Get Outdoors Day is time for "healthy, active outdoor fun at sites across the nation." Find a sponsored event near you or check out descriptions of other events around the country for some ideas for you to do at home: www. NationalGetOutdoorsDay.org.

13. ACT OUT YOUR FAVORITE STORY

Storytelling can involve acting out movements in a very animated way. What is your child's favorite book? Chances are she knows the words by heart. Is there a story that takes place outside? Help your child use her outdoor space to tell her favorite story to you with big movements and an expressive voice. When she's ready, she can invite a loved one to listen to it. Use the patio, deck, or porch as an outdoor theater for her performance.

14. BUILD A LOG CABIN WITH STICKS

I love Lincoln Logs, and we've even taken them outside to use. But, if you don't have Lincoln Logs or don't want to take them outside, collect sticks and build tiny log cabins. You can build one house together by stacking sticks in a square shape and then laying sticks horizontally for the roof. Pluck flower heads from nearby weeds or wildflowers and decorate your house. You can keep going and make a whole town! Experiment with different shapes, such as rectangles.

15. TAKE YOUR PERSPECTIVE UP

A cousin in France once said that she did a sociology experiment in college and asked people to purposefully look up and around for a day. What she found was that it not only opened people's perspective to the physical beauty around them, but also to a more psychological openness of possibilities. Take this idea into play with your child when you walk outside and start looking at what is above your eye level, and take turns pointing out what you see.

Schedule in Some Time for You

We spend so much time focusing on summer activities for our kids that it is also important not to forget time for us to decompress with some fresh air. Alone or with a loved one, enjoy a daily bike ride, walk, laps at the pool, or something new that you've always wanted to try. If it's hard to get away, ask a neighbor or friend to watch the kids while you take a break with an activity outside, then you can return the favor for them. We all deserve to relax; you just have to make sure to do it!

16. TASTE FRESH HERBS!

One of the things I love about having herbs is plucking some to taste or rubbing the leaves and smelling them every time the kids and I walk by them. Years ago, I learned the hard way that mint should be in a container (it invaded our side yard). The stevia plant is a natural sweetener and fun to taste. Easy herbs to start with like rosemary, sage, thyme, and oregano come back every year (they are perennials) and are great for cooking too. Whether in containers or in the ground, plant herbs in full sun (at least six hours) and well-drained soil.

17. PLAY IN THE SPRINKLER AND WATER THE GARDEN

If it's been dry and you need to water your garden or grass, plan to do it when the kids can put their bathing suits and sunscreen on and romp around in the spray. If you don't wait for them, you may arrive home from work one day, kids in tow, and find that they'll hop into it fully clothed!

18. LOOK FOR BUGS

Even if you don't like bugs, it's fun to explore and see what you can find. Ants: check. Pill bugs: check. Spiders: check. Now, see if you can discover something that you've never seen before or look for the most colorful bug. If you're inspired by your exploration and would like to know more about what you might have seen, you can look at www.WhatsThatBug.com.

19. HAVE SOME SURPRISE OUTDOOR FUN ON FATHER'S DAY

Have the kids plan an outdoor extravaganza by asking them what outdoor games they'd like to play with Dad. The kids (with or without your help) can draw a picture of or write the name of each activity on a separate piece of paper, with a note about why your child likes playing that game with him. Then, put the pieces of paper in a hat and let Dad pick! If you don't get to all of the games on Father's Day, he can draw another activity the next time the kids have special time with him.

20. GET A SPRAY FAN

I rarely suggest an activity that involves buying things, but I am a huge fan of those battery-operated portable spray fans that you can fill with ice water to spray. The reason I like this portable spray fan is that it gives you some relief outside when it is hot, which could be starting now or really intensifying, depending where you live. I learned about the spray fan when a dad brought one to soccer practice for his son on a hot evening. A way that you can have the same cooling experience without having to buy something is with ice packs, washcloths in icy water in a cooler, or ice water in a clean spray bottle.

21. CELEBRATE SUMMER'S ARRIVAL WITH THE SOLSTICE

Revel in the longest amount of daylight, which occurs on or around the first day of summer. Let the kids play in the fresh air longer; perhaps even eat outside, and continue with bedtime stories on a blanket. Share with your kids what you love about enjoying the longest daylight of the year and ask them to offer what they like best about it too.

22. ATTRACT A HUMMINGBIRD

Plant perennials that attract hummingbirds, such as red cardinal flower (Lobelia cardinalis), coral trumpet honeysuckle (Lonicera sempervirens), bee balm (Monarda), beardtongue (Penstemon), and coral bells (Heuchera). While hummingbirds are attracted to red flowers, they are really looking for flowers with the most nectar to refuel. Want to know more about hummingbirds? Check out www. wild-bird-watching.com.

23. WASH THE CAR TOGETHER

Staying cool and doing something functional is always helpful, and kids love to help wash cars. Splash around and clean the car at the same time, while also working together and spending time as a family.

24. SWAP TOYS WITH A NEIGHBOR

Share an outside toy with a neighbor and ask to borrow one of theirs for the day. For example, remote control cars are perfect outside toys! If you don't have one, ask to borrow one from the neighbor for something new to do. Then you can let the neighbor pick an outside toy of yours that she would like to enjoy for a day.

25. DIP YOUR TOES IN SOME SAND

You may or may not be heading to the beach anytime soon, but when was the last time you all felt the warmth and fun of dipping your toes in some sand? No sandbox or beach? Pick sand up at the hardware store and pour the sand in a shallow plastic tub. Now roll up your pant legs and dive in together! Extend your outdoor play with measuring cups (scoop in the sand and pour for pretend cooking) and hiding objects in the sand, such as shells you collected from the beach last summer. Replace the top on the plastic tub and keep it in the coat closet for the next time your child wants to play in the sand outside!

26. SLEEP UNDER THE STARS

Don't forget! The last Saturday in June is the National Wildlife Federation's Great American Backyard Campout (www.backyardcampout.org). Pitch a tent in the backyard and sleep out there with the kids. Then try a real overnight camping trip within an easy drive of your home. As dusk falls, watch for interesting creatures. If you're lucky, you might see lightning bugs or even bats! (Keep bug spray on hand, in case the bugs include mosquitoes!) To cushion your back, I highly recommend a thick sleeping pad under your sleeping bag or even a portable air mattress.

Teach Your Kids to Deadhead

I recently saw an article about teaching children "the art" of deadheading, or pruning faded blooms. Honestly, unless we're talking about trees and shrubs (best left to adults with sharp pruning tools), there is nothing complicated about plucking faded blooms from your flowering annuals and perennials. I encourage my kids to do it whenever they see a dried-up bloom. Just as weeding regularly will help vegetables grow in the garden, removing dead flowers from your plants will encourage new growth. This can be done by hand, or supervised, with kids' scissors.

27. LOOK FOR AN AERIAL BATTLE

At this time of year, the kids and I tend to notice small birds engaged in battle with a larger bird in the distance overhead. Many times, we see these amazing displays of nature when we are in the car, but it's not limited to that context. Turf battle? A hawk hunting for newly hatched baby birds? We're never sure what it's about, but we see these aerial battles many times during the season. Keep watch on the sky; can you find one?

28. WATCH FOR WILDFLOWERS

Along the side of the road where grass has not been mowed or in state parks in fields and meadows, you'll start to see wildflowers. Just as you hunt for twinkle lights in the winter, think about watching for flowers in patches of tall grass as you go about your daily routine. Consider revisiting them through the summer and watching how they change. Are the flowers the same month to month? Are there butterflies? Which are your favorites? If there are flowers you would love to have in your outdoor space, look up your local native plant society, where you may find photos and names of these plants. You can also explore native plants by state at www.Wildflower.org, the website of the Lady Bird Johnson Wildflower Center.

29. BLAST THE BALL

With kids around, chances are that you have at least one ball that is lightweight and super bouncy. Take turns seeing how high you can kick the ball into the air. Stay alert and keep your head up, though, to avoid getting bonked in the head! You can even try to catch the ball as it comes down.

30. LOOK INTO THE WATER

Even if you don't have your fishing gear, when you come across a body of water, whether a puddle, creek, stream, pond, lake, river, or ocean, you can look closely into it and find another world of activity. Find its clearest area; what do you see? If you're patient, can you find a fish? After a rainstorm, go to areas where the water has collected to see what insects or frogs are drawn to it. Want to make it a science experiment? You can even test water quality. Learn more at www.FriendsOfTheCreeks.org.

july

Take your celebrations outside!

In July, the days are long and there's still plenty of time to do all the things on your family's summer wish list. My advice? Hurry up and try those activities you haven't done yet, before the whole summer zips by. Think about combining indoor and outdoor activities, like a trip to the museum followed by an outdoor picnic on the grounds.

Can you believe how many children's birthday celebrations take place in the summer? After a while, they blend into each other. There are a handful of companies that specialize in hosting these parties—including Pump it Up and Gymboree Play and Music. For my son's birthday, I decided to borrow that brilliant model—gathering kids and their parents together in an exciting place for two hours of fun activities—but to simplify it way down and bring it outside. We organized an outdoor party with a nature walk that was fun for kids *and* their parents. Our birthday bash included a simple picnic lunch, cake and fresh-roasted s'mores, and party favors with an outdoor theme (toys including balls, bubbles, and plastic pails and shovels). It was the most low-key, successful gathering

I've ever had, and a lesson about the possibilities for future birthday parties.

July Activities

1. BRING WATER PLAY TO YOUR INDEPENDENCE DAY

All across the country, families will set up barbecues and picnics for Independence Day, enjoying outdoor time with friends and loved ones—with or without fireworks. For something extra-special, how about a water extravaganza? You can set up a great, kid-friendly party without springing for a huge, self-inflatable water slide. My family hosted a fantastic party in July with a plain blow-up pool and two slip 'n' slides that we connected together. Toys that we bought for the party became favors for kids to take home: beach balls, inner tubes (donuts), and fans that spray water (great to have on hand for a summer walk, by the way). The food was set up inside, away from bugs, but the entire party was held outside. Kids and their parents stayed well beyond the two-hour schedule.

2. GRAB SOME INFLATABLE WATER TOYS

Even without a pool, lake, river, or ocean nearby, inflatable water toys can be used for countless summer games. See how many activities your kids can come up with using a beach ball and an inner tube. Kicking, bouncing, throwing, rolling, racing, and hopping—my own kids thought up quite a few.

3. TEND THE HOT SUMMER GARDEN

In the July heat, get the kids to help you water the plants

every day. And remember that some early summer perennial flowers like yarrow (achillea) fade after a month or so. Take your children back to the plant nursery for gorgeous late-summer blooming perennials such as purple coneflower and yellow rudbeckia (black-eyed Susan) that flourish in the heat and also attract butterflies. And if you want to plant your own pumpkins, now is the time to do it. They can take four months to grow! If you're putting in more annuals, let the kids pick the colors and patterns; for example, alternating purple and white petunias.

4. SPRUCE UP YOUR GARDEN, FOURTH OF JULY STYLE

A Fourth of July garden makeover is a great way to decorate for a party, have an activity for kids, or make gifts of red, white, and blue flowers in a decorated pot. My five-year-old wanted to make a flag on a pot and we brought out our paints and markers from his craft room, spread out newspaper on the ground, and let him create. I like small plastic pots with drainage holes because they are lightweight and hold moisture well. Think about sun-loving annuals like red geranium, white petunias, and tiny blue lobelia. Small patriotic pinwheels can be placed in the pot and are a great outdoor party favor for the kids. Remember that pots that sit in the sun all day are best watered in the morning to keep moisture from evaporating.

5. MAKE SOME SOLAR S'MORES

Did you know that you can make s'mores outside even

without a campfire? This great idea to teach about solar energy comes from a third grade teacher. Simply make your s'more (place a large marshmallow and piece of chocolate between two graham crackers), wrap it in a piece of aluminum foil, and set it in the sun for ten minutes. Unwrap it and voila! The s'more is ready to eat. Think of wrapping up this treat in your backpack on a hike. When you stop to eat your lunch, place the wrapped s'more in the sun. By the time you're done with your sandwich, dessert is ready!

6. HOLD A BEE SCAVENGER HUNT

According to Buzzle.com, there are nearly twenty thousand types of bees. My children and I noticed at least a few different kinds that I had never seen before when our allium bulbs bloomed at this time of year. Take a stroll and see how many different kinds of bees you notice. Did you know that honeybees pollinate one-third of the food we eat? Häagen-Dazs is encouraging families to plant gardens to help our important pollinators: www.HelpTheHoneyBees.com.

7. HAVE A SPONTANEOUS POTLUCK OUTSIDE

My new friend Donna told me about how whenever she and her neighbors called their children to come inside for dinner, the kids begged to stay out longer. So, one night, she and her neighbors took dinner outside. Spontaneously, dinner became an informal potluck, sharing among families what they had prepared or had on hand. The kids got to eat and the parents got to visit.

> ### Need to Buy a Child's Birthday Present?
> ### Consider an Outside Toy
>
> Many of us think of something classic and educational
> for children's birthday gifts, whether books or intro-
> ductory board or card games. And of course, there is
> the latest favorite character or toy of the birthday girl
> or boy that makes birthdays fun. But outside toys are
> a great idea too, whether it's bubbles, bouncy balls,
> small tennis racket, an introductory plastic set of golf
> clubs, or gardening gloves and seeds. Kids love to
> play with their birthday presents, and a great way to
> share the fun of the outdoors is with a toy that helps
> take them outside.

8. VISIT A FAMILY-FRIENDLY CAMPGROUND

Two years ago, I traveled cross-country from D.C. to Denver
with my girlfriend Janelle, her two-year-old triplets, and my
boys, staying in family-friendly campgrounds along the way.
But you don't have to go on a cross-country trip to find a
family-friendly campground. Find a local campground and
visit to see what they have to offer. Many times, there are a
pool, a mini-golf course, and fire rings to roast s'mores.

9. PLAY CROCODILE

This one is adapted from a tennis camp game, and it works
whether you have two people or ten. The "coach" throws
a tennis ball across an imaginary line to each person standing and lined up in a row facing the coach. If you do not
catch the ball each time the coach throws it to you, you lose

a limb (e.g., put an arm behind your back, then stand on one foot or sit down, until finally you have no limbs left and are out). The last person left wins and becomes the coach.

10. FIND A NEW PLACE TO SWIM

Last summer, I took a couple of afternoons off to take the kids to new places to swim outside that didn't cost a dime. A simple Internet search showed me where I could find a shallow swimming hole, or naturally occurring pool of water, along with important safety tips (www.SwimmingHoles. info). Another search turned up a swimming beach on a river and a swimming lake with a campground, both less than two hours away. With life jackets on the boys, water shoes, and mom's rules for where they could swim, we all had a blast!

11. CREATE YOUR OWN DRIVE-IN

Our family loves watching movies together. If you have a laptop computer that plays DVDs, you can take nighttime movie-watching outside. Put the laptop on a table; sit in some lawn chairs with some popcorn, and you've got yourself a drive-in. Want a bigger screen? If you have a projector to hook up to your laptop, you can project the movie onto a sheet hung between two trees.

12. RACE IN THE WATER

Kids and adults can have much different skills when it comes to swimming. Where the water is about waist-high for your kids, suggest a running race from one side of the shallow end to the other. The water resistance makes this type of race a great workout for everyone. Another option is to wear inflatable pool rings and kick your way across to the finish line.

13. THROW OBJECTS TO RETRIEVE

Even if your children aren't old enough to dive below the water's surface and retrieve an object, there is a role for them in sitting on the edge of the water and throwing the object into the water for older kids to find and bring up. Dive torpedoes/rockets, rings, sticks, and plastic action figures (to name a few) can provide lots of entertainment.

14. HOLD ONTO THE BALL

We play this game in the pool, but you could also play it on the grass with a large exercise ball. The object of the game is to see who can balance on top of the ball the longest. Even if you fall over in the pool, if you are still holding on, try to use your body to get back in position on top of the ball. Adults can help little ones play and balance.

15. READY, AIM, ROLL!

One day, our ten-year-old friend Gil was rolling a tennis ball between our dog's legs and giggling. That quickly led to other attempts to roll the tennis ball and precisely hit different targets with increasing difficulty. Use whatever ball you have on hand, aiming at whatever is around you.

16. NAME YOUR TOP THREE GAMES AND PLAY ONE

Looking for something to do? Ask your children to name their three favorite games, then play one of them. For example, the informal poll I took with one girl and two boys yielded: "Soccer. Tag. Hide-and-Seek." "Hide-and-Seek. Hula-Hoop. Climb Trees." "Tag. Hide-and-Seek. Playing Catch." They then decided to play tag.

17. FIND A SHORT HIKE OR BIKE RIDE

By short, I mean a maximum forty-five-minute round-trip route. Ask your neighbors and friends about their favorite trails that are close by and nicely shaded. It could be around a lake, in the woods, at an arboretum, or along the road. Then try it! Don't forget to take water with you.

18. PLAY FAUCET TAG

My kids call this game "toilet tag," but I am officially giving it a new name that has nothing to do with the potty. If you get tagged, you have to freeze with your legs shoulder width apart and one arm out. Then, your teammate can unfreeze you by going through your legs and putting your arm down (turning off the water).

19. HAVE A SPONGE AND BUCKET RACE

This activity is a kid favorite from field day at the end of the school year, when students play games outside most of the day. The object of the game is to see who can move water the fastest from one bucket to another with a sponge. Rather than needing two buckets for each team, you can play with plastic bowls or cups. Each person or team has one bowl full of water, one empty bowl, and a sponge. When you say, "Ready, set, go!" you fill the sponge with water, run to the empty bowl, and squeeze the water into it. The first child to transfer the water from the first bowl to the second wins.

Have a Pick-Your-Own Party

July can bring some delicious activities in the form of picking fruit, such as blueberries, blackberries, cherries, or peaches. Invite some friends to have an excursion with you. Or, if you need to plan a summer birthday party or family reunion, consider this activity followed by a gathering at a picnic shelter or nearby swimming lake.

20. CREATE SOME ICE CUBE ART

Draw with ice cubes on the sidewalk. If you think about it the night before, drop some food coloring in each ice cube mold and you'll have different colors for your sidewalk ice cube art!

21. MAKE A RING TOSS GAME

Take some tin foil and shape it into a ring. Then, give each child one ring and select objects outside that they can try to throw the ring onto, such as a shrub or tree branch, a doorknob, your arm, or your foot. When you're done exploring, you can put a stick into the ground for a more traditional ring toss.

22. USE YOUR BUCKET OF BALLS

At our house, we have accumulated a lot of balls over the years, from small to large. Make up one game using all of them at once or a series of games with each type of ball you pick up. For example, try to throw each ball and hit a selected target (as simple as a piece of paper on the ground at a manageable distance based on the ages of your children). Or, hit the ball with its appropriate companion accessory (tennis racket for tennis ball, golf club for golf ball, foot for kick ball, etc.). See what games you create together!

Beat the Heat and Humidity

You know the saying, "If you can't beat 'em, join 'em." You can still find ways to get outside and stay comfortable when the heat and humidity seem too much. My formula is shade, a breeze, and water. You can create any of these things and enjoy them independently or together. Create a breeze on a shaded bike path, put some ice water in a bowl and take your child's bath toys outside for some water play, or kick a ball under the shade of a tree. Carry a water bottle filled with ice and water at all times.

23. LIE UNDER A TREE AND LOOK UP

I love to do this with my sons in our hammock, but you don't need a hammock to enjoy the shade and the view up into a tree from underneath. The silhouette and pattern of the tree's leaves against the sky is beautiful. Want to get even comfier? Lie on a blanket and bring a pillow for your heads.

24. PLAY MOSQUITO

Inexpensive spray bottles are a great alternative to squirt guns. When it's hot out, your kids can fill them with water and chase each other (spraying "mosquitoes"), offering an inviting spray that's sure to generate some happy squeals of excitement. Make sure the bottles are clearly labeled "Water," and keep them with your sunscreen or outside toys.

25. PLAY HULA-HOOP BALL

A spin off of kickball, it's easier for kids to accumulate points in this game because the three bases—Hula-Hoops—are bigger. The pitcher rolls the ball for the child to kick, just like in kickball, but every time a child lands in a Hula-Hoop, she gets a point. If the child is tagged with the ball before reaching a hoop, she is out. After three outs, you switch sides.

26. ESCAPE THE HEAT OF THE DAY

Think of things within your daily routine that you can do early in the morning or late in the evening to enjoy the coolest parts of the day. Ride bikes or scooters. Color or read a book outside. Play a board or card game on a blanket. Maybe even skip rocks on the water or go fishing.

27. INVENT PRODUCTIVE USES FOR SQUIRT GUNS

Sooner or later, your child will have some contraption that shoots water. Direct the water in ways that don't involve spraying you: encourage your child to write her name or letters on the sidewalk, squirt the water into the air like Old

Faithful, squirt your toes, or, at the pool, squirt a ball along the surface of the water.

28. CREATE A TREASURE HUNT

Everyone loves to find treasure! Create clues to find treasure in your yard or in the park. Hide something and write down clues in advance or inconspicuously drop some change or bags of snacks behind a tree as you walk to the playground for a surprise game on the way back. Make up one to three clues spontaneously based on what you see around you, such as, "Go to the biggest tree, then under the bench, and look around the trees beside it." A treasure hunt could be a fun new way to have your kids find the allowance they've earned!

29. FIND AN EAR OF CORN ON THE STALK

Find a field of corn (or head to your own garden if you planted corn in May). Take a close look and find a fresh ear of corn growing. I had seen plenty of cornfields in my life, but never looked closely to see how an ear of corn grew until I was an adult! Buy some freshly picked corn from a roadside farm stand and take it home to cook and eat.

30. RATE IT!

Just as we rate puddle jumps in spring rains, in the summer, we rate the kids' cannonballs. If your kids are younger than four, they might not yet be jumping in the pool, knees tucked, and making the biggest splash. What you can do though is find something else to rate, such as their ability to hold onto the side of the pool and blow bubbles while they kick their legs. The desire to perfect their score keeps them going longer and longer!

31. RIDE ON THE WATER

At the beach, many of us love to play in waves. A great family activity is boogie boarding, where you hold on to a soft but firm board and ride the waist-high waves to shore. It's easy for parents to help a child and maybe even do it side-by-side once both are comfortable. If the child is able to hold onto the board but isn't ready for boogie boarding, you can pull them along the water at the edge of the beach, similar to pulling them on a sled.

august

You *can* have fun in the (sweltering) sun.

In many parts of the country, August is hot, buggy, and humid. Think shade. And use the longer days (more daylight hours) to work around the oppressive heat. Continue to take advantage of the coolest times—early mornings and evenings—when outdoor activities like family walks, bike rides, ball tosses, and working in the garden are more enjoyable.

As summer winds down, ask the kids to help you make a list of their favorite summer activities. Do some of those things again—before school schedules intervene! What haven't you tried yet this summer? How about putting up a lemonade stand or visiting an amusement park? As the days pass, your family can add to the list, writing down some fall activities that you are already looking forward to. Preserving these ideas while they're fresh in your minds will give your family a valuable list of activities you can return to, and build on, over the next year.

In the garden, you can still add another plant or two. Last year, the milkweed plants we purchased in August had monarch butterfly eggs all over them. The kids watched twelve caterpillars grow from teeny tiny to huge. Watching them build their chrysalises and hatch into monarch butter-flies was mind-blowing.

And find water! Whether you visit the beach, a swimming hole, or the local pool, it's cooler by the water and there are plenty of activities to enjoy. On quick trips to the beach and a swimming hole, my boys discovered sand crabs and salamanders and they had a great time digging in the sand and soil. Organize a fishing or sailing trip and bring along someone with a bit of experience. Try making your own fishing poles and learn how to cast a fishing line. Even if not everyone fishes, an outdoor picnic can be enjoyed by the whole family.

August Activities

1. SET UP A LEMONADE STAND

Let the kids run their own business for an afternoon, setting up a stand in a shady spot and selling cold drinks to the neighbors. What could be more appealing than iced lemonade or iced tea on a hot summer day? And it will give the kids a practical lesson in buying and selling, customer service, and math (figuring out the profits for the day).

2. BUILD A VOLCANO!

Next time you're at the beach, make a sand volcano. My friend Eli loves doing this in winter in California; she even organized her son's third birthday party around the activity, combining it with a pirate theme. Mound the sand and dig a hole in the middle. Put some baking soda inside, pour some vinegar into the hole (little hands can do this with a small squeeze bottle), and watch the volcano bubble with lava! For the finale at the birthday party, they put a Mentos in Diet Coke (with the kids standing back) and it really shot up.

3. SWEEP THE STOOP

When it's hot outside, sometimes we need some fresh air but don't want to move around too much. Think about sweeping the stoop with your child. Kids love to help, and you may even have a child-size broom. The repetition of the sweeping can be very relaxing, and it's something that may need doing!

4. GRAB A BUCKET OF WATER AND...

You may want your bathing suits on for this one! Fill a bucket with water and ice (optional), and add some fun items before you head outside. For example, pick all of one thing (e.g., one or more sponges for tossing back and forth) or combine a lot of different soft things in the bucket, such as bath toys, a washcloth, and an old T-shirt. Then head outside and play! For those not afraid to get totally wet, you can play a variation of duck, duck, goose, where you toss a wet washcloth or sponge back and forth, each time saying "duck" until one of you shouts "goose," tossing the sponge back and running from the other person, who has to chase and tag the other person with the wet sponge. Have towels ready by the door for drying off.

My Top Picks for the Beach

Don't leave home without these items for your trip!

- Kite
- Bouncy ball for kicking back and forth in the sand (beach balls tend to fly away!)
- Small plastic shovels and sand castle molds (take a small suitcase or large bag with what you have from last season so you don't have to buy new ones)
- Recycled plastic grocery bags for collecting shells
- Boogie board
- Coast Guard–approved life vests

5. PLAY ICE CUBE GAMES

Fill one cup with ice cubes, grab a couple of spoons and an empty second cup, and head outside to play some games. Toss the ice cube back and forth with your hands. Have a spoon race, each person balancing an ice cube in a spoon. Toss the ice cubes from afar into the empty cup. Time how long it takes for an ice cube to melt on the pavement; then see if you can melt one faster (e.g., with warm water or a magnifying glass).

6. HAVE FUN WITH WATER BALLOONS

Sometimes filling water balloons is an outdoor activity in itself, using an attachment for water balloons on a hose, filling them, tying them closed without popping, and placing them gently in a bucket. Once you're ready, play balloon toss, where two people try to catch the balloon without letting it pop. Smaller children can try to gently toss and catch the balloon on their own. If you have a large supply of balloons and at least two willing participants, try playing splash ball. The object is to get the other person or team wet by throwing the balloons at the other team's feet.

7. TOSS AND SPRAY A BALL

Here is a different way to water the grass that is fun for the adults too. Toss a lightweight ball in the air and spray it with a hose, trying to keep the ball in the air. The kids can play in the spray and try to catch the ball as it makes its way to the ground.

8. COLOR AND MAKE A FAN FROM PAPER

On a hot day, a paper accordion fan can provide a helpful breeze. I usually forget about hand-held fans until I get to an outdoor event like a state fair and businesses are giving them away. Have your child color a scene on a piece of paper (front and back if they have the patience) and then, a half-inch at a time, fold the piece of paper to one side, then the other, repeating until the entire piece of paper has alternating half-inch folds. Tape the bottom together so your child can hold it and fan it back and forth to create a breeze.

9. CREATE YOUR OWN WATERPARK

Slip 'n' slides are wonderful alternatives to a community pool. Join a neighbor's slip 'n' slide with yours on a small hill and the kids are sure to have hours of fun. Want to create your own waterpark? Combine the spray of the slip 'n' slide with an inflatable pool and bring out inner tubes and beach balls for lots of games in the yard.

10. HAVE A CUP CONVERSATION IN THE SHADE

Make a telephone outside. Pick two trees from which to have your conversation and measure a piece of string that will reach between them. Take two plastic or paper cups, poke a hole in the bottom of each and tie a knot at each end of the string (you can tie the string around a small stick inside the cup if the knot keeps slipping out of the cup). Sit under your trees, then one of you talks into the cup while the other holds it to his or her ear. Be sure the string is pulled tight! Can you hear one another?

11. DROP AND SPLASH

Fill a bowl with cold water, then sit on the stoop or sidewalk and drop some bath toys one at a time into the bowl and see how they splash. Which make the biggest splash? What happens when you increase the height from which you drop the object? If you have some squeeze bath toys, fill them with water and see who can spray the water the farthest.

12. COLOR IN THE SHADE

One evening we had eight kids on our stoop, sitting in the shade and coloring pictures for their parents and grandparents. All I did was bring out paper and crayons and the kids did the rest. They sat and talked and created. The best part was seeing the amazing creativity and care that they put into their drawings!

13. HAVE A LITTER PICK-UP RACE

Head out into your neighborhood, each with a plastic bag, and see who can pick up the most litter in ten minutes. This is a great way to do something that helps your community and makes you feel good too. Carol McCloud wrote a great book, *Have You Filled a Bucket Today?*, that my kids read in preschool. The book is a great conversation starter for others things you can do to help people, your community, and Mother Nature.

14. MAKE HOMEMADE ICE CREAM

While I remember summer weekend afternoons when my parents would make homemade ice cream, I don't have that much patience or time. FamilyFun.com has an easy five-minute ice cream recipe. The only thing you might need from the store is 6 tablespoons rock salt. Place rock salt and ice (half full) in a one-gallon sealable plastic bag. In a second, smaller plastic bag, combine 1 tablespoon sugar, ¼ teaspoon vanilla, and ½ cup milk. Close the small bag and place it inside the large bag. Close the large bag and shake it for five minutes or until you have ice cream! Get a spoon (or two) and enjoy it straight from the bag.

15. MAKE PICTURE FRAMES FROM SHELLS

One summer at the beach, after we washed the shells we

collected and were looking for something to do, we headed to the local craft store to pick up small wooden picture frames and craft glue. Back at the condo, we laid out newspaper and glued shells to the picture frames. The final result made great gifts for family of photos of the kids at the beach.

16. COLLECT AND COMPARE

You can do this with shells, leaves, sticks, rocks—any item from nature. Collect five of one thing, such as shells, and compare the shape, texture, size, and color of them. Then, repeat the process with something else, such as rocks. Afterward, you could even contrast the shells to the rocks for interesting conversation.

17. PLAY LEAF TIC-TAC-TOE

Make the tic-tac-toe grid from sticks (or draw it in the dirt). Then, each player picks five of the same leaf for his or her playing pieces. For example, my son picked maple leaves and I picked oak leaves. Now you're ready to play tic-tac-toe with two different types of leaves instead of Xs and Os. Three of the same leaf in a row wins. You can do the same at the beach with shells, drawing the grid in the sand.

18. SKETCH THE LANDSCAPE OUT THE WINDOW

Is it too hot? What I love about this idea, developed by my husband, is that you draw, together, the landscape on one piece of paper. Use crayons, markers, paint—whatever medium is at your fingertips. Then sign your combined work of art.

Look for Summer Clearance Sales

Children's Adirondack chairs, patio furniture, and beach toys may be on sale soon. Think about what functional and beautiful items may spruce up your outdoor space, as well as what you can use year-round. For example, pool rings are great for rolling down hills and tubing in the snow in the yard. Hula-Hoops are wonderful year-round too. See what you can inexpensively add to continue the outdoor fun as the seasons change.

19. CLIMB HIGH AND TRY GEOCACHING

Head to the mountains for cooler air and try geocaching, a worldwide movement of finding outdoor treasure boxes and family fun. You even get to take something from the treasure box and leave something behind. Find out from your local outdoor retailer if you can rent a hand-held GPS, which is needed for this activity, or borrow one from a friend. There are also geocaching apps for smart phones. Learn more at www.geocaching.com.

20. MAKE A FAMILY SAND CASTLE

A lot of families do this, and if you haven't, I highly recommend it. When you are at the beach, make it your objective for the day to make the biggest sandcastle together that you've ever made. You can start with gusto, then take breaks. What is wonderful about this is that there is so much discussion about wonderful ideas that are then seen to fruition. Will all of your or your children's ideas be structurally sound? Maybe not, but you can give them a try and experiment.

21. PLAY MARCO POLO AT THE POOL OR AT HOME

We all know Marco Polo in the pool: one person closes their eyes and says "Marco," while relying on hearing to find and tag the others who say "Polo." What if you played this in the yard? You may want to set ground rules for the perimeter and speed at which people can try to get away (e.g., walk). Consider designating a coach to help direct you ("right," "left," "straight," "turn around") when you're trying to tag someone.

22. PLAY A GAME FOR A GROUP: SHARKS AND MINNOWS

When you get together with your family, this is a great game to play. It's a favorite at soccer practices all across the country. Two people are the sharks; everyone else is on the other side and has a ball; they are the minnows. The minnows start dribbling or gently kicking their balls to make it to the other side. The sharks approach the minnows and if the sharks kick your ball away from you, you have to join them. The object of the game as a minnow is to make it to the other side. This game is also fun to play on the beach.

23. PLAY PICNIC BLANKET BOCCE

Roll some grapes like marbles and get them close to something: your drink, a strawberry, the plate. Whoever's grape is the closest wins.

24. HARVEST YOUR SUMMER VEGETABLES

About now, you'll be harvesting your summer crop. What did your family grow and love? Carrots, tomatoes, bell peppers, squash, corn, beans? Ask your children what they loved best about growing their own vegetables and talk about soon planting more: leafy greens for fall such as collards, kale, Swiss chard, and scallions. You can also repeat cool season vegetables from spring such as peas, lettuce, and radishes.

25. HOST A COLLECTIVE BEACH TOY EXTRAVAGANZA

Invite the neighborhood kids to combine their beach toys for an hour or two of fun in the yard or at the park (ask parents to label them with names). Children will likely make up games right away with so many toys to choose from. If not, suggest they build a maze lined with toys, or line up the blow-up pool rings and hop through them. See how many games of volleyball they can get started with the beach balls or create designs on the ground with the hand shovels.

26. FIND A MONARCH CATERPILLAR

On the Internet or in a book or pocket guide to native plants, look up pictures of the different types of milkweed and then go look for some. What might you find on the undersides of milkweed plant leaves? You may find yellow, black, and white striped caterpillars of monarch butterflies, which lay their eggs on milkweed, which young caterpillars eat before forming their chrysalis. One summer, we met a boy who had found ten caterpillars by looking for milkweed throughout his trip. He would look at each caterpillar in its habitat, then gently hold it, before putting the caterpillar back where he found it. What an amazing discovery!

Share Your Summer Veggies

It's always nice to give a gift, and why not from your garden? You can take some of your harvest to neighbors or even bring it as a hostess gift to a party. There are also great programs, such as Plant a Row for the Hungry, where you or your school can pledge to plant an extra row of vegetables to donate to a local food bank. Learn more at www.GardenWriters.org.

27. PLAY HOPSCOTCH IN THE SHADE

Find a tree along the sidewalk that offers nice shade when you want to play. Get out your sidewalk chalk and play hopscotch with your child. Label the first square "1"; the next two squares on top of "1" are "2" and "3"; then the fourth square is "4" and the pattern continues up to "10." The object is to throw a pebble on each number sequentially to ten and back, hopping on one leg, and then standing on one leg to retrieve the pebble and hop back. You can place both feet on "2" and "3," "5" and "6," and "8" and "9" respectively.

28. MAKE AN ISLAND

My friend Tina played this growing up in Norway. You and your child stand far apart, each holding a piece of chalk. Then each of you draws a circle around yourself (these are your two islands). Your job is to connect them and make one big island. Go to the edge of your circle and draw another circle until your circles eventually touch. Make up a story about your big island. Who lives there? What do you like to do to have fun on your island? What do you eat? If you could eat only one thing and drink only one beverage, what would they be?

29. MAKE SHADE

Give your kids some old sheets or blankets and tell them to make some shade outside. They can drape the sheets over lawn furniture and make a fort, just like they do inside. Have them clean it up at the end of the day, or you can let them sleep outside under it!

30. GO AND WATCH WHAT YOU WANT TO LEARN

What do you want to learn to do as a family? As I discussed in the March chapter, I learned a huge amount about fishing while exploring a local park with my boys and watching a mom teach her young daughter and son how to fish. Now I want to learn how to rock climb with my family. I'll go to a popular entry-level trail and watch with my boys to see how it looks before signing up for some lessons.

31. CELEBRATE!

On occasion, my younger son will say to me, "Mom, I think we need to have a celebration." And I ask, "What do we need to have for our celebration?" Decide together how to say good-bye to August and your favorite summer activities. A picnic? A barbecue? Play in the sprinkler? How about all three? Decide what will make your end of August outdoor celebration special.

fall

I have to admit—last year, my family's transition to fall was rocky. The summer's endless stream of gorgeous days with long daylight hours made it easy to get the kids outside. And for the first time in my life I treasured every moment of it, despite my busy work schedule. But now that my boys were heading back to school with its hectic pace (including homework and soccer practice) I suddenly panicked. How could I preserve our precious outdoor time while the boys struggled to adjust to their new schedules? Would autumn escape from us in the blink of an eye? Sending my kids back to school for indoor learning felt contrary to my dream for my sons—to let them "be outside and grow."

I tried to imagine what I could do to keep my New Year's resolution without jam-packing every weekend with trips to the apple orchard, pumpkin patch, and fall festivals, and without putting too much pressure on the kids during the week. Soon, the days would start to feel short and dark again, and I was already feeling the gloom.

But then it hit me—we had managed to have great outdoor time in the winter and spring, so it was definitely possible! I would return to walking the kids to school, stopping by the park on the way home, having picnic dinners, inviting the kids to do homework on a blanket in the grass, initiating family walks, and saying yes as much as possible when they asked me to play outside.

I also learned to embrace "Plan B." To paraphrase the Robert Burns poem, the best laid plans of mice and men (and busy mothers) often go astray. When weekend traffic jams ruined my attempts to take my younger son into Shenandoah National Park to see the dramatic changing of the leaves, we found our own special viewing at a tiny local park. This was a great lesson to me. Your family can have a rich and wonderful experience wherever you are. Flexibility and patience can lead you to discoveries that are off the beaten trail, and these can turn out to be more satisfying than your original plan.

One day last fall, while biking through my neighborhood, I had another epiphany. I was pedaling along, taking in the wild grasses on the side of the road, which were turning from green to yellow, and I reached a footbridge over a creek. I stopped and listened. I heard acorns fall intermittently, saw an occasional leaf wafting to the ground. The evening sun created long shadows of the surrounding oak trees, and I felt a kind of euphoria as time stood still. Connecting with fall wasn't about all the places my family could race to. The rich changes that happen in nature are going on all around us, every single day. We just have to be willing to stop, look, and listen. I vowed to be open to stopping with my children and husband whenever they wanted to notice the details of the season.

And the very next day, on our walk to school, we did stop. My five-year-old knelt down to examine tiny snail shells in two different spots. The first time he stopped, I caught myself worrying that we would be late. But then I remembered my vow on the footbridge, and the second time he stopped, I realized that even if we were five minutes late to school—which we were not—it wouldn't be the end of the world. Now, if we are ready for school a few minutes early, we go ahead and start walking. That way we have more time to discover things along the way.

After giving so much thought to kids and the natural world, I wondered if the teachers at our local school were providing enough educational outdoor time. That's when I developed my free guide, "Outdoor Classrooms: The Basics," from talking to other parents and educators who had started successful school learning gardens. Even if you don't have a lot of time to give, providing your child's teacher with this information and some seed packets is one way to encourage teachers to plan lessons outside. I lead outdoor lessons at the local elementary school, taking kids out to the school garden where they not only experience firsthand the plant life cycle and the relationship of gardens to people and wildlife, but also write and illustrate stories about what they see. Giving children the tools to draw and write about the outdoors is a wonderful, creative activity. It teaches them to look closely, and to share their observations with others.

When Can You Plant?

As a general rule of thumb, you can plant perennial flowers, shrubs, and trees whenever you can dig in the soil: spring, summer, or fall (i.e., when the ground is not frozen). I plant these anytime from March to November, continuing into the fall when the temperatures are in the fifties because it gets me outside when the temperatures drop. Except for annuals (including vegetables and some herbs that live for only one season), in late fall through winter your plants will be dormant (at rest). Seed packets will have instructions on the packaging with regard to the proper temperatures for germination (sprouting).

Throughout the fall, our garden continues to give us pleasure. And when time is short, spending even a few minutes out there can be rejuvenating. Just as catmint (nepeta) and salvia are butterfly-attracting staples for the spring and summer, the aster is a butterfly-friendly staple for the fall garden. In September, our asters are bursting with color and surrounded by countless butterflies in all sizes and colors. Native to North America, the aster will fill your garden bed with green in the spring and summer, and then burst into show in the fall. In late May or early June, I cut back the foliage by as much as two-thirds (mums too, by the way), to ensure a fuller, sturdier base for the fall blooms. I also examine our perennials. If any of them are outgrowing their spaces, I divide them (literally split them in half with a straight shovel) and transplant one half to another spot. It's a great way to expand the garden without having to buy new plants.

What to Grab on Your Way out the Door

I try to have in the car any diversions that are productive and help pass the time when we are away from the house, such as:

- A deck of cards, for example UNO
- Picnic blanket
- Snacks and water
- A ball
- A Hula-Hoop
- Rebecca Plants Curiosity Cards (of course)

september

Back to school: an outdoor perspective on learning

While some schools are back in session in August, September still feels like the official start to the school year. The kids are excited (and maybe a little nervous) about new teachers and subjects and seeing their classmates again.

School schedules mean less time for outdoor adventures, so find opportunities before and after school to get outside while the weather is still mild. And remember that learning about nature is a lifelong process that happens at home as well as in the classroom. For example, this is a great time of year to invite beneficial wildlife into your garden by providing a water source (bird bath, fountain, or a small pond) and native plants that provide food, shelter, and places to raise young. Our family garden has a small water feature and native plants like the aster (a perennial that provides nectar for butterflies); trees such as evergreen foster holly; and shrubs, like the deciduous Virginia sweetspire, that add beautiful color in the fall.

All year round, my family sees so many cool things in our yard, including skinks (a lizard with a black upper body and an electric blue tail), praying mantises, grasshoppers, and frogs. Sometimes we play "I spy," where one person names a creature they have spotted and it's up to the other players to spot the creature too. After we planted a native climbing red trumpet honeysuckle (Lonicera sempervivum) right outside the kitchen window, we had daily visits from a hummingbird!

September Activities

1. PLAY FOUR SQUARE

Really, any game with a bouncy ball will do. We often play four square before setting out for school. Using chalk, draw a quadrant of four squares on the pavement and bounce the ball back and forth to one another, technically one bounce at a time and staying within the squares. There are more rules, but my kids change them all the time! Have the kids make up their own rules.

2. PLANT COOL-SEASON VEGETABLES

When the temperatures are back down in the sixties and seventies, plant easy-to-grow cool-season vegetables like collards, kale, spinach, scallions, lettuces, and radishes in the ground or in containers. You can even replant peas at this time. Don't worry if you're not a fan of these vegetables. When they are ready to harvest, you can try them, alongside your kids!

3. THROW A POT PAINTING PARTY!

Gather some paints and brushes, along with a few old plastic or terra cotta pots for planting, paper towels, a small bucket of water, and a trash bag. Cover your workspace with newspapers to protect it, and then help your kids decorate the old pots with festive new designs and pictures. My boys made a friendship pot for their friend who was moving in a month, complete with their handprints and signatures.

4. MAKE A LEAF SCRAPBOOK

Leaves change colors at different times depending on where you live. Your kids can start to learn about the leaves around you and track their changes with a leaf scrapbook. For example, start with collecting five different leaves for leaf rubbings, then label them. Look up the names online or ask a neighbor if you don't know. Later, when the leaves start to change color, collect the same five leaves and glue them into your scrapbook, noting the date. With each addition to your scrapbook, ask your child to tell you a story about your experience that you write (or they do if old enough).

Easy Ways to Help Your School

Even if you don't have a lot of time to offer to your child's school, what about offering to lead one thirty-minute outdoor activity for your child's class? No time? Mention these easy lessons to the teacher for parents who volunteer in the classroom:

- Plant a pattern of bulbs (fall)
- Create bagel bird feeders (winter)
- Plant peas in cups (spring)

5. DO HOMEWORK OUTSIDE

Your kids may or may not have homework, but the concept applies for anyone. Invite a friend to join your children in laying out a blanket in the grass and taking workbooks, journals, reading, or coloring. My kids actually get their homework done faster and complain less if they have a friend come over and do homework at the same time. Best of all, the kids can play outside when they are done; I love to keep the fun going with a picnic dinner.

6. FIND A FALL CROP TO HARVEST

Back-to-school time is a wonderful time to tour a local farm, see what is growing, and have another pick-your-own adventure with a crop like fall raspberries. Call before you go, as weather impacts what is available and when. No farm? Head to the local farmer's market and explore what you can taste together.

7. SCHEDULE OUTSIDE TIME INTO YOUR ROUTINE

Let's face it; our schedules are busy. Many times, if I don't schedule something, it doesn't happen. Schedule in fifteen minutes before you leave in the morning to let the kids have outside playtime if they get ready quickly. Do the same in the evening; for example, stop by the playground on your way home with the kids. Keep a picnic blanket in the car and on occasion you may even want to pick up sandwiches for a picnic dinner.

8. MAKE A NATURE CONTAINER

Kids love to collect things from nature, and my boys are sad when they can't bring something they've collected inside. They are afraid it will get lost outside. A nature container is a perfect solution. Give your child her own plastic container with a lid where she can keep what she finds. The container can be stored in a closet by the door or in the garage, and she can easily grab it when she wants to play with her nature objects outside. Take a tip from the National Wildlife Federation: and hang a clear shoe organizer on the back of a door so your children can put treasures into the convenient pockets and see what they've collected. (Visit their website at www.BeOutThere.org for more ideas.)

9. FIND WONDER IN A SMALL PAIL

My neighbor's girls love their plastic child-sized pails. The girls are constantly taking their pails around the yard and collecting things to look at: blades of grass, acorns, pine needles—anything from nature. They then sit with their objects and look at them under a magnifying glass and invite others to sit with them and look at their discoveries. Have each of you take a pail or basket (even a plastic bag will do) and independently search for ten minutes in your surroundings to see what you can find. Then, come together to share your discoveries and do a little show and tell.

10. PLANT BUTTERFLY-ATTRACTING ASTER

Aster is a perennial (it returns each year) and native to North

America; best of all, butterflies love it! We had seven orange monarch butterflies and many more smaller butterflies frequent four aster plants. Plant aster in full sun in the yard or in containers; just remember that containers in full sun will need water daily. In the ground, water two to three times a week after planting, then gradually wean back watering to one time a week if it hasn't rained. Not only will your kids love the butterflies, the neighborhood kids will love them too!

11. VISIT A LOCAL NATURE CENTER

When my kids were two and four years old, we didn't have much nature around us, so we went to find it and we loved the local nature center. It was a good twenty-minute drive from where we were, so whenever I was near that area we always stopped by to see up close turtles, frogs, and snakes. A recent Internet search with my county name and the words "nature center" turned up five that I didn't even know about! Sometimes we just need to remember to do a quick Web search to discover the great resources available to us.

12. BOUNCE BACK TO SUMMER

Pretty quickly, we can get sucked into the stress of our commute or the summer vacation high finally fading. What made summer so great for you? Write down the best three things about your summer; ask your kids the same question and add their answers to the list. Then decide a simple thing that you can do in the moment to make it feel like summer, whether it's walking barefoot in the grass, having a glass of lemonade, or taking a family walk in the fresh air.

13. PLAY FOUR STICKS

Each of you grabs four sticks to see how many different letters or shapes you can make. For example, I saw a three-year-old make an *E* with his four sticks. You can also make a rectangle. What else can you make? If you combine your sticks, how do your creations change?

14. RECIPROCATE WITH AN OUTSIDE PLAY DATE

Neighbors are wonderful; we try to help one another as often as possible in ways that complement our schedules and give our kids some fun. For example, invite your neighbor's children to come over for thirty minutes of playtime, which gets your kids and the neighbor's kids outside and running around. I always have a pitcher of water or juice on hand and a stack of small cups, as well as a big tub of pretzels for a snack. If we pick up some kids for a walk, I put juice boxes and a large bag of pretzels in a backpack. Soon, your neighbors will reciprocate. These short outside play dates are a great way for the kids to get exercise and for you to get things done (or run around with them too).

15. ASK WHAT THE KIDS WANT TO DO AFTER SCHOOL

According to the Afterschool Alliance, "Each afternoon across the United States, 15 million children—more than a quarter of our children—are alone and unsupervised after school," and 8.4 million children are enrolled in an afterschool program. Regardless of where your kids are after school, ask them what they like to do after school and what they would like to do more of. Often our personal resources limit what our kids can do, and these questions may provide inexpensive ideas for your child's afterschool program or a way for our children to become involved in the community or activities that don't cost any money. For example, your child may want to spend more time outside at aftercare or there may be a nearby Boys and Girls Club for afterschool activities.

16. FIND A LOCAL MARINA

Watch boats come and go, see birds fish, and soak in the breeze at a local marina. You don't have to own a boat to appreciate their beauty; just lay down a picnic blanket for a snack while you watch. There may even be canoe or kayak rentals that you choose to come back to another day.

17. SEE AND LEARN ABOUT THE MONARCH MIGRATION

Are you seeing orange monarch butterflies yet? Head to your garden, a neighbor's, or the local Cooperative Extension master gardener's butterfly garden and see if you can spot some resting their wings on their journey to southern California or Mexico. Check out a book from the local library to read while you're there, such as *Hurry and the Monarch* by Antoine O Flatharta and illustrated by Meilo So.

18. MAKE TIME FOR REFLECTION

On occasion, I will suddenly notice a beautiful reflection of puffy clouds in a window I pass by on the street, or my kids will notice their reflection in my sunglasses. Raindrops, puddles, or a nearby pond or a creek offer beautiful reflections too. Play a game where you count how many reflections you can see. Play the game whenever you are together and keep a running tally. The kids can draw pictures of their favorite reflections or describe them to a friend.

19. FEEL THE BREEZE

During a sailing lesson for my television series, *Get Out of the House*, the sailing instructor asked us to close our eyes, feel the breeze, and then sense from which direction the breeze was blowing. At any moment and wherever you are, you and your child can do the same. How do you check and see if you're right about the direction of the wind? Take a small leaf from the ground and hold it flat on your palm. See in which direction it flies away!

20. USE THE SPACE IN BETWEEN YOUR BUSY SCHEDULE

We're always running from one place to another. The next time your family is out of the house and waiting around, whether in between practices or outside the doctor's office, make the most of it. For example, kick a ball, spin around, or climb a tree. No space to roam? You can ask one of my Curiosity Card questions, such as, "What could we build with what is around us right now?" While waiting outside a doctor's office with me one evening, my son made sailboats from leaves and acorns.

21. SAY HELLO TO FALL: PUT MUMS IN CONTAINERS

Move summer-blooming perennials out of pots and into the ground, then put colorful fall mums into your containers. The mums can be kept in the containers all winter. Then, in spring, you can clip off the dead branches and replant the mums in the ground (repeating the cycle of putting newly bought perennial flowers into your containers). The mums may return next fall and bloom again. Simply cut back the mums' green foliage in late spring by as much as two-thirds to ensure the stems grow strong enough to support the flowers that bloom in the fall.

Plan a Scenic Train Ride

Think ahead to how you want to experience the changing leaves this season and do an internet search for scenic train rides in your state. Chances are a scenic railway will offer many trips at different times of the year. For example, a scenic railway in my area not only offers fall foliage trips, but also bald eagle tours. The train route offers many things to see that provide lots of conversation, including farms, waterways, and glimpses of wildlife along a route we rarely get to see.

22. MAKE FISHING POLES WITH YOUR FAMILY

Pick a glorious September weekend and take the whole

family—grandparents, aunts, uncles, and cousins—fishing. Make your fishing poles together beforehand! All you really need is a long stick, string, and a hook to put at the end. When my family went fishing for the first time, we cut some four-foot lengths of bamboo (my mother-in-law's yard has too much of it) with a saw. Next, we drove a nail through one end of each pole with a hammer (a rubber mallet is great for the kids to use). Then we removed the nail, threaded through some fishing line (scotch tape folded together on the end of the fishing line holds it straight so you can thread it through the hole), and secured the line around the end of the bamboo pole with a knot. You can have one of your kids determine the length of the line by pretending to be a fish! A foot from the end of the line, hook a bobber (so you can see when the fish bite), attach a weight a couple of inches below the bobber, and tie a hook to the end of the line. You can purchase lures that look like bugs or worms or take a hand shovel with you and the kids can dig up the worms for you!

23. CLIMB SOME ROCKS

On two trips with my kids, one to Sioux Falls, South Dakota, and the other to Central Park in New York, something very similar created at least an hour's worth of fun: rocks. These boulders, ranging from two feet to ten feet tall, were the perfect diversion from the ordinary. The children were drawn to "rock climbing," as they called it, hopping from rock to rock, and even sliding down. "Mom, you've gotta try this!" they called. So hesitantly, then happily, I joined in on the fun.

24. FIND AN ADVENTURE PLAYSCAPE

The Maryland Zoo has a giant tree slide and lily pads; Ski Roundtop in Pennsylvania has an outdoor zip-line for tots; the Morton Arboretum in Lisle, Illinois, has a four-acre children's garden with lots of spaces to explore. Many gardens also offer tree house exhibits that make you feel like a kid again. Find a nature-inspired playground in your area or for your next road trip at www.KidsPlayParks.com.

25. "FORCE" SOME FAMILY FUN

Are the kids bored or getting on each other's nerves? Take a family vote about what you want to do. My husband and I suggested we vote on *A*, fishing, or *B*, renting a canoe. Each of us cast our vote on a small piece of paper, and my boys both wrote down *A* and *B*: to go fishing on a boat! Our forced family fun was so fun that we were out all day together and officially hooked on fishing. If you need ideas for which of your area parks offer fishing, boating, biking, hiking, or camping, enter your zip code at www.DiscoverTheForest.org.

Create a Secret Garden

My younger son Warner was thrilled when we made him a secret garden. We chose a spot hidden between some trees, and he made a border with rocks he collected from the yard. We transplanted some flowers from another part of the garden. As a parent, I liked his hidden spot because it gave him a place to dig that didn't upset my yard's curb appeal. All he needed was his imagination and a hand shovel. By transplanting or dividing existing plants, we didn't even spend any money. As the season progressed, both Warner and Harmond added plants to the secret garden, and they are still in charge of weeding and watering it.

26. HAVE A CHILD'S-EYE VIEW

Go on a walk with your child and simply watch what they watch; see the world through their eyes. I remember when my younger son was twenty-four months old and we were on vacation in Florida. What normally was a five-minute walk to the beach took thirty minutes because he would walk a foot and then bend down to watch something on the ground. Back then, I was frustrated with wanting to get to the beach. Three years later, I got a chance to follow his lead through Paris, and his curiosity and wonder inspired me to learn alongside him at his pace.

27. SIT, BREATHE, AND OBSERVE

Sometimes you don't have to do anything outside for the impact to be great. Find a comfortable place to be still and watch the nature around you. Sit for as little or as long as you can together, taking deep breaths and simply watching what is around you. If it's easier for your children, have them bring a notebook and colored pencils or crayons with them to sketch what they see. At the end of your quiet time, talk about what you notice.

28. CREATE AN OUTDOOR GAME ROOM

I created a checkerboard on a flat stone, drawn with a permanent marker, and two sets of different colored rocks for playing pieces that I gathered from the ground. But you don't have to be crafty to take games outside. Horseshoes, a bean bag toss, croquet, or your favorite board game like Chutes and Ladders on a blanket will do just fine.

29. SHOW OFF YOUR SCHOOLWORK OUTSIDE

Have the kids do an outdoor show and tell of their latest schoolwork for you and family members. Gather outside and your children can take pride in describing their new learning experiences and art. Top it off by having the children show you the outdoor games they play every day—make sure you take part!

30. PAY TRIBUTE TO YOUR BEST EXPERIENCES

My children and I recite our "three great things" before bed each evening. When you are together, ask each of you to say your three great outside memories since the start of school. Decide which of them you are going to do next, or draw or write about them in tribute to making more special memories in the fall.

october

Beyond the pumpkin patch: Bring that enthusiasm and wonder home!

Carving pumpkins, taking the kids apple picking, and watching the leaves take on gorgeous shades of red, orange, and yellow always gives me a renewed appreciation for the abundance of nature. There are many ways to share this sense of joy with your kids, and one of the best is cooking.

There is something very satisfying about eating what you harvest from your own garden. It encourages kids to be daring and try foods they are dubious about. I think that having our own garden is one reason why my younger son got interested in cooking.

I'm not much of a cook. I make a mean healthy salad if you want to drop by for lunch, and I have figured out some great one-pot meals—stews and soups loaded with protein and vegetables—that don't take much effort and give us more time to spend outside. But my husband is gifted in the kitchen, and I was thrilled to discover that my five-year-old takes after his dad in the cooking department. In October we are still harvesting our cool-weather vegetables and my son's signature dish is an amazing alphabet chicken noodle soup!

He makes it with a rotisserie chicken and chicken stock, a bunch of veggies, and of course alphabet pasta. With a little help from me or my husband, Warner makes this delicious soup for family and friends when they come to visit.

Even if you buy your veggies from the grocery store, flavoring them with herbs that your kids have grown from seeds or seedlings makes them taste extra-delicious. And it's easy to grow herbs on your windowsill, no matter where you live.

October Activities

1. PICK APPLES AND PUMPKINS

Visit a local orchard and pick your own apples. For the young cooks in the family, making applesauce or apple pie from the fruit they picked can be loads of fun. Pumpkin carving is another seasonal favorite, and once your jack-o'-lanterns have been created, you can toast the pumpkin seeds in the oven. Even better, pick that pumpkin from a farm's pumpkin patch—the sea of pumpkins is an incredible sight, and the kids get to really pull and twist to pick their own! You may want to bring a pair of gloves to grab the prickly stems.

2. PLANT A PATTERN OF PANSIES

Here's an educational activity that I did with my son's kindergarten class that's easy to replicate at home: plant a pattern. How? Decide on the colors you want to plant and the order of the pattern. For example, my son wanted to plant orange and purple pansies in an alternating pattern. We even snuck in crocus and daffodil bulbs into the alternating holes as well and put the pansies on top of the bulbs, knowing the bulbs would come up the next spring. What a great way to maximize the return on the hole you dig!

3. HEAD FOR THE WATER

As the seasons change, there is something very calming about the water. Regardless of whether you head to the beach off-season, you can appreciate the soothing nature of water in whatever form is closest to you: a creek, stream, pond, lake, river, or ocean. Take a snack, sketch pad, or a picnic and a ball and spend some time together.

4. LISTEN TO A LITTLE NUT MUSIC

If you have oak trees around, are the acorns falling? Or do you notice other trees with nuts on the ground? Collect some nuts and see how many sounds you can make by putting them in recycled cans or tying them up in plastic bags and shaking them like maracas. My neighbor's girls like putting sand between two acorn caps and shaking it by their ears to hear the sound; then they proudly remove one acorn top and offer you a "sip" of their pretend milkshake!

5. MAKE YOUR OWN BUBBLES

My neighbor, Abby, recommends this recipe from the Exploratorium in San Francisco (www.exploratorium.edu) for tons of bubble fun. Her three girls, ages four, six, and nine, use up bubbles quickly, so she refills the containers when they run out. She makes a large batch in a recycled plastic margarita bucket from summer vacation that has a spout to easily refill bubble bottles: 2/3 cup Joy dishwashing soap, 1 gallon water, and 2 to 3 tablespoons of glycerin (available at a pharmacy).

6. SPOT A PREDATOR

It's interesting to look at an insect or an animal and think about why it may be attracted to that spot. For example, a ladybug may be eating aphids on your plants. A praying mantis, which my children and I usually see in early autumn, may be hunting the ladybugs that show up in droves at that time. Head out the door and talk about the first insect that you notice on the ground. Why do you think it has chosen that location? Then, learn more about their habitat and what they eat. Check out www.Insecta-Inspecta.com and www.A-Z-animals.com.

7. CREATE THEN HIDE PUMPKIN FACES

Not everyone carves jack-o'-lanterns. My neighbor created a brilliant fall activity that she used for a birthday party but can be done at any time, especially if each child brings a pumpkin. Each child paints a face on her pumpkin (you could use washable markers too). Then, take and print photos of each face or draw quick renditions on paper. While the kids are busy with snacks, hide the pumpkins. Give each child the picture of their pumpkin that they need to find. It's fun to ask the kids to name their pumpkin too!

Bring the Outdoors into Your Office

Office plants brighten a space and help clean the air around you. Philodendron, golden pothos, and spider plant have been known to eliminate indoor pollutants. GreenUpgrader.com recommends three essential green plants: areca palm, mother-in-law's tongue, and money plant. Also consider natural seasonal decorations that you would normally include in your home, such as mums, aster, or other cut flowers from the garden, and small pumpkins and gourds.

8. HAVE "BATTING PRACTICE"

No bat or baseball required. One day when I was in a bad mood my husband made this game up with the kids and I was outside smiling in a heartbeat, wanting a turn. All you need is a very lightweight bouncy ball. For example, a beach ball is perfect. Straighten your arms, clasp your hands together, and batter up! The bigger and lighter the ball, the easier it is for even the littlest kids to have a turn.

9. MAKE A FAIRY ALTAR

My friend and professional gardener Leigh has little girl guests often on her property. What do they like to do? Besides planting or tasting some veggies or berries, they like to make fairy altars or tiny spaces that honor the fairies that help Leigh in the garden. The girls organize berries, leaves, sticks, seedpods, moss, and grass on rocks throughout the garden for the fairies to enjoy.

10. WATCH FOR BIRDS FLYING SOUTH

At home, orient yourself with which direction is south, and be on the lookout for birds migrating south for winter. Which birds migrate? According to the National Wildlife Federation's website, waterfowl, raptors, hummingbirds, and songbirds fly south, some as far as the tropics. The National Wildlife Federation's Wildlife Watch can help you determine which animals to look for. Visit www.nwf.org/WildlifeWatch.

11. HEAD BACK TO THE FARMER'S MARKET

Explore the cool-season vegetables. Ask the farmers when they start growing certain vegetables to become familiar with when you might want to try growing your own produce. Find your favorites and if you haven't planted yet, try to grow them! See how long you can extend your growing season with a floating row cover on top of your raised vegetable bed to keep frost off the plants. Available at your local nursery or through an Internet gardening supply company, a floating row cover can be secured with landscape stakes or rocks.

12. TRACK THE CHANGES IN THE SEASON

Pick a day every week to go out to the same spot with a notepad and pencil and write about or draw the changes you notice that are taking place in nature. Or keep a notepad and colored pencils in the car for your child to sketch the changing landscape as you travel around. Have them present their art to you, and write down their story beside their art if they can't do it themselves.

13. HAVE A FALL HARVEST CELEBRATION

My friend sent me wonderful photos of her temple's Sukkot celebration in Denver, Colorado. Families decorate an outdoor pergola with evergreen branches and beautiful white twinkle lights. Children trace leaves and cut out the shapes on red, orange, and yellow paper and glue them in a circle to form fall wreaths that are hung for decoration. Gourds and pumpkins serve as centerpieces on the table. Consider bringing a fall harvest celebration to an outdoor dinner with your family. The weather may be just right to enjoy fall crops and decorations with a meal outside.

14. HUNT FOR NUTS AND SEEDS

We all know acorns, but how well do we know them? Look at their different sizes and how they differ from the other nuts or seeds you find. Are there flower heads that have dried out and gone to seed? Look closer at them to see the individual seeds that provide food for birds. On the cold, wet ground, you may even catch an acorn sprouting to grow an oak tree. Once home, create designs with your collection.

15. BUILD A STICK TUNNEL

Collect short sticks and twist them securely into the ground, crossing the tops to create an arch. Repeat over and over and see how long of a tunnel you can make. Grab some small cars from inside and try to send them through to the other side!

Imagine Your Ideal Month

What does your ideal October look like within the context of your family, work, and schedule? What are you doing? How are you enjoying your time as a family? What part of your daily routine can you take outside that would help ease the stress of the day? The answers could be as simple as an evening walk or bike ride, making time for a fall festival that you missed last year, or getting the kids to the playground more often. See how you can improve your month with a little more fresh air.

16. FOCUS ON THE SOUNDS

Have a challenge with your kids and see how many sounds they can hear outside. Ask them if they can hear more sounds the quieter they are. Listen first for a minute or two, and then start to identify the sounds. What animals do you hear? If you don't know the names of the animals, what do the children think they might look like?

17. HEAD TO THE COUNTRYSIDE

Oh, how I wished I lived right in the mountains, like in Park City, Utah. Regardless of where we have chosen to live, we can take a weekend day or two and head to the countryside, where there are scenic roads, state parks, and hiking trails. As my friend Jennifer does each year with her husband and three boys, ages two to eight, you can rent a log cabin and enjoy time together, catching grasshoppers, taking walks in the woods, and watching the sunset over the foothills. Or take a tent and sleeping bags and try an overnight camping adventure!

18. HAVE YOUR FIRST S'MORE OF FALL

We love our fire pit, and use it every chance we get from fall through winter and early spring. Even if you don't have a campfire, keep supplies on hand for an outside s'more snack. Simply heat a piece of chocolate and a large marshmallow between two graham crackers in the microwave for ten seconds and take your warm treat outside to enjoy!

19. GRAPH THE CHANGING LEAVES

This is a fun activity that introduces graphing to your kids. Each of you takes a bag outside and picks ten to twenty leaves of different colors. Then, represent in a bar chart on paper, with different color crayons, how many of each color you have; for example, one green, four brown, three red, two yellow. To make a graph, draw a grid on a piece of paper and color in vertically the number of squares to illustrate the number of leaves of that color (e.g., color one square green, four squares brown, etc.). As an alternative to paper, you can group and vertically stack the leaves on the ground in order from most to least.

20. MAKE 'EM RAKE LEAVES

You likely won't have to make your children rake leaves (they'll want to do it themselves!) although they may need your help focusing to complete the task after playing. Playing in the leaves is a great time for some candid photos of your kids in their exploration or maybe a time to ask a neighbor for a family photo. No yard? No problem! Head to the local park to kick together piles and have a jump. Or simply take a walk in the park and kick the leaves along the trail.

21. DISCOVER WHAT'S IN THE SHADOWS

I love waking up to the sunrise, and as I walk to make a cup of coffee I notice the light coming through the windows and making beautiful shadows on the walls. Put on hats and jackets and take your coffee outside (the kids can have hot chocolate or warm Ovaltine as we do in our house). What shadows are cast in the early morning light (e.g., shadows of the trees on the ground)? Discuss how the shadows might change as the sun moves west throughout the day. What shadows might you see at the end of the day? When you get home, take a look together and see how the shadows are different.

Cook with Your Fall Harvest

Spinach, kale, collards, squash, scallions, and fresh herbs. Thinking of fresh vegetables is making me hungry for a healthy fall meal. Since I'm not a gourmet cook, I love either eating my veggies raw in a salad or sautéed in olive oil and garlic.

Rachael Bender, author of the cookbook *From Field to Table*, recommends thinking outside the box for fall meals. How about a butternut squash quesadilla with onions, garlic, red pepper, and Cheddar and Monterey Jack cheese? Or a spinach, mushroom, and garlic quesadilla topped with mozzarella cheese? One of the greatest things about quesadillas is that your kids can help you assemble them. And when the kids help prepare dinner, they are more likely to eat all their veggies!

Another great use for fall vegetables is on pasta. Sauté your leafy greens with olive oil and garlic, add some pine nuts and good Parmesan cheese, mix in with pasta, and you've got a quick and easy dinner that is sure to please. You can a make unique pesto sauce by using arugula and walnuts instead of the standard basil and pine nuts.

Oven roasted veggies with olive oil can make a delicious side dish for any meal.

One of the best things is to get your kids involved in growing and harvesting the vegetables. They are more willing to try new foods if they can proudly boast, "I grew that!"

22. SKIP ROCKS

Find some water and spend time selecting the flattest rocks you can find and trying to skim them across them water so they bounce or skip multiple times. I usually have to try about twenty before I finally have the right flick of the wrist to skip a rock on water. My kids usually can do it before I can!

23. PLANT GOLDENROD

Cooler temperatures make fall a great time to plant Goldenrod (Solidago). A favorite of butterflies, this sun-loving feathery gold perennial flower is native to North America and makes a beautiful show in fall, standing two to three feet tall. I even had a monarch chrysalis hang from one of its sturdy branches. Ask your local nursery about the best native plants for your area. The bonus of native plants, whether trees, shrubs, or flowers, is that they are more likely to thrive in your climate without fuss and extra care beyond what Mother Nature has to offer.

24. CHECK ON YOUR GARDEN

It's time to check on the seeds you planted in early September; is there salad ready to harvest for dinner yet? If you started pumpkin seeds in July, what happened? Did they grow? Now is a good time to head outside with your children and a garden journal and colored pencils for each of you. Start noting what worked well with your vegetable garden this year and what you'd like to do differently next year.

25. SAY "BOO!"

"Booing" neighbors after dark is a great way for the kids to get some fresh air and giggles by sneaking around the neighborhood and leaving anonymous baskets of treats or fresh produce from your garden for your neighbors. Of course, adult supervision and glow sticks are required!

26. PLAY MUSICAL HULA-HOOPS

Invite a couple of neighbors to each bring their Hula-Hoops and put them in a circle. Then, a child or you can get one of your musical instruments and play a tune or beat a drum. When the music stops, the players have to hop in the center of a Hula-Hoop. Whoever hops in last removes a Hula-Hoop and is out. The remaining players repeat the game until there is only one player left!

27. JUMP THE RIVER

Take two sticks and place them parallel or across from one another on the ground; the sticks represent the edges of the river. Then, ask your child to jump across the river. After each jump, the sticks move farther and farther apart (the river gets wider). Keep attempting jumps until someone lands in the river!

28. HOP TO IT!

My children play this game in P.E. at school. Make sure you're on a soft surface such as grass, then each of you puts a ball between your thighs. Pick a point to hop to and let the race begin! If it's hard for your child to hop forward while holding the ball with his or her legs, they can hop in place and practice balancing.

29. MAKE ROCK ART

This idea, from GoExploreNature.blogspot.com, is about collecting as many rocks as you can and then making a design on the ground. Equal parts exploration and imagination, each of you takes a small pail or plastic bag and starts walking and collecting. Of course, you'll be stopping and noticing and talking along the way. Whenever you're ready, have a seat and start creating. You can bring in other elements of nature, such as leaves and sticks, if you'd like. The website creator's son made the design of a tree on the ground from his rocks, and even "hung" shells and animal figurines from it.

30. FIND A BLIZZARD OF LEAVES

Have you ever noticed how each leaf falls differently? A ten-year-old girl in my neighborhood loves to run in a "blizzard of leaves" when the gusty wind blows them all around. Point out to each other the cool spinning, floating, or diving leaves.

31. CELEBRATE HALLOWEEN

What are you doing for Halloween this year? It may be warm enough for a spooky Halloween party in the yard, or cold enough for a table made of snow on which you can set out the treats. In a friend's neighborhood, families like to gather at the end of their driveways with a portable fire pit or chiminea to socialize outside while the kids come around the neighborhood for treats.

november

Planting flower bulbs is the easiest
family planting activity ever!

When the temperatures are in the fifties and sixties and the days get shorter, our hibernating tendencies start to kick in. You can fight this with invigorating outdoor activities like walking, biking, and playing sports outside.

And guess what? If the ground is not frozen, there is still planting to be done! November is my time to put in bulbs that will come up in the spring, Yes, we're talking about delayed gratification; it takes months for the bulbs you plant in November to emerge from the ground or from outdoor flower pots. But when they do, your investment of time, energy, and hope will be well worth it. I already know what will happen when those tiny green tips start peeking through the snow in early spring. My kids will race into the house yelling, "Mom, the flowers are coming up!" What a lovely way to inject some excitement into the cold weather.

Why not take the kids over to their grandparents' house (or an aunt, uncle, or family friend's house) for a bulb-planting party? It's a wonderful gift you will enjoy twice. First, it's a fun excuse for a family visit that includes outdoor time;

and second, when the bulbs come up in the spring, you can take the kids back to check on them.

Of course, one of the best things about November is Thanksgiving! Backyards and local parks are the perfect place to go "shopping" for holiday decor. And it gets people out of the house on Thanksgiving Day. Have each guest make his or her own place card out of natural objects they find outside. My five-year-old made a stunning place card with a giant leaf, a hummingbird's nest, a flower seed head, acorns, and a rock. It was fun to see what Grandma, Grandpa, and other family members did with their Thanksgiving Day findings too.

November Activities

1. PLANT SPRING-FLOWERING BULBS

I like to plant my bulbs after Halloween, when there aren't as many activities competing for my family's time. Here are three options for planting your spring-blooming bulbs:

1. Pick a spot in your yard that's near the front or back door, or outside a window the kids can easily see out of. Dig a trench in the soil that's a few inches deep and scatter a whole bag of mixed bulbs—early- to late-spring blooming—in the trench. Do a quick check and point as many bulbs root-side down as you can. The rest will find their way.

2. Dig holes between existing plantings. I placed a combination of four different deer-resistant bulb varieties

side-by-side in each hole to get the maximum result, such as white daffodil, purple grape hyacinth, white leucojum, and pink wood hyacinth.

3. If you don't have a yard, don't worry, you can have bulbs too. Just plant them in a flower pot and keep them on your outdoor stoop or balcony. Plant pansies directly on top of the bulbs, and the bulbs will sprout right through the pansies in the spring.

2. GET READY TO FALL BACK

The first Sunday in November marks the time to adjust clocks back one hour, gaining an extra hour of sleep (if your kids actually sleep in). While you'll most likely be waking up in the dark, you get to watch the sunrise. What a wonderful way to start the day with your family. Look up when the sun will rise and plan to see it together. Older kids can start tracking when the sun rises and sets over the next month as daylight is gradually shorter and shorter until December 21, the day with the least amount of light.

3. HARVEST YOUR OWN SEEDS AND STORE THEM FOR PLANTING SEASON

In mid-fall (and other seasons too) watch for flowering plants whose blooms have dried and produced seeds. Invite your kids to collect the seeds, dropping them into individual paper envelopes and labeling each envelope so you'll remember what's in it. In the spring and summer (and even fall for some perennials), pull out the envelopes and plant those seeds outside. There is something magical about harvesting your own seeds. It's also a great gift for someone or a way to save money on seeds the following year! Any seeds not harvested can be left on dried flower heads as food for the birds.

4. LEARN MORE ABOUT WHO IS GETTING READY TO HIBERNATE

Bats, frogs, snakes, and bears find places to hide out all winter, but you don't! According to www.SaskSchools.ca, skunks, badgers, raccoons, squirrels, chipmunks, and beavers are "Nappers and Snackers," finding a warm place for winter, but still active at times for food. Look around and see if you can spot animals getting ready for winter: squirrels making warm nests high in trees and collecting nuts, holes in logs where animals may live, you may even notice that birds are getting more plump in preparation for winter.

5. SEE WHAT'S ON SALE

It's that time again! Head to the nursery as a family and see what is on sale for you to add to your garden. Garden accessories? A favorite shrub or tree (for example, your state tree)? Don't forget to look for berry bushes and fruit trees too.

6. WATCH AIRPLANES TAKE OFF AND LAND

Head to your local airport to watch the amazing choreography of airplanes taking off and landing. November is a great time to do this, since it gets you out of the house.

A small regional airport may be closer to home and get you closer to the planes. Bring a ball or kite with you for some off-season fun. Your airport fieldtrip may even serve as a launching point for stopping by the playground on the way home.

7. DISCOVER WHAT IS DORMANT

Dormancy is a plant's method of hibernating for the winter; leaves die back and the plant sleeps and sprouts again when the weather warms up. For example, where I live the grass is dormant in winter; my perennials are too. Deciduous trees and shrubs lose their leaves. Evergreens, such as pines, may lose some leaves or needles, although they quickly return. Go outside and notice what flowers, shrubs, and trees are going to sleep for winter, storing energy to return next spring.

8. MEASURE THE LEAF FALL

Pick a patch of woods, then go outside with a yardstick to measure the height of the layer of fallen leaves. Pick two to five days on your calendar over the next three months to measure again the height of leaf layer in the same spot. Is the layer of leaves smaller? If so, the leaf layer has likely started to decompose. Each time you measure, clear away some leaves to look at the soil underneath the leaf pile. Note your child's observations in the notebook; maybe even take some photos. Over time, does the soil look darker and richer as the leaf pile decomposes?

Why November Is My Favorite Month

Every time I get to my birthday in mid-November, I look around at the leafless trees and laugh that the landscape around me doesn't necessarily look like anyone's favorite month. But I love how I spend my time. My family roasts s'mores several times a week with the kids' friends, we ride bikes almost every day, and we get to watch the leaves dancing in the wind. In sweaters and jackets, we're having a good time, and the outdoors is my place to host family and friends as the number of gatherings picks up. Blankets are always on the chairs outside so people can visit comfortably in the crisp air.

9. CREATE AND MARK A PATH IN THE LEAVES

Make believe that you need to mark your trail through the leaves. What will you use? Rocks? A string? Popcorn? Peanuts? All the balls in your closet? Create a trail, mark it, and follow your trail back. Don't forget to put away the string or balls when you're done! The popcorn or peanuts can be left as a snack for the squirrels or birds.

10. PLAY GHOST IN THE GRAVEYARD

Kids are brilliant at making up countless renditions of tag; there could probably be a whole book on the subject of tag alone. A family of three children, ages five to ten, brought Ghost in the Graveyard to my attention. For the first game, someone is picked as the "ghost," and that player hides. Those left count to ten from base and then go look for the ghost. When one of you sees the person who is it, you yell, "Ghost!" and try to run back to base without being tagged by the ghost. If you are tagged before hitting base, you become the ghost and the game begins again.

11. PRETEND AT THE PLAYGROUND

Invite your child's best friend to the playground and they can act out their favorite book, TV program, or movie on the play set. When my mother was a child, she loved to pretend she was Peter Pan with her friends, and they would use the jungle gym as their fairy world. Your kids can do the same as they pretend to be their favorite characters.

12. MAKE YOUR OWN FOSSIL

Take a small box, such as the cardboard wrapping for a bar of soap. Make sure both ends are taped shut and remove one side of the box. Go outside and mix up some dirt with water to make thick mud and put it in the box. Press objects, such as shells, rocks, leaves, or sticks into the mud and bring the boxes with mud inside to dry. When mud is dry, you can remove the objects to reveal your "fossil," the imprint of your object.

Do You Need a Change of Pace?

Sometimes our days can seem like a movie played over and over again. What can you do to change it up for everyone in the family? Here are some ideas:

- Head to a favorite park or walking trail that you haven't been to in a while.

- Invite family friends over for a drink, and the kids can play together while the adults reconnect.
- Visit an outdoor sculpture garden, arboretum, or zoo to spot wildlife.

13. PLAY PICKLE

My five-year-old cousin Reagan introduced me to "Pickle," which he plays in the summer at baseball camp. As it gets colder, it's a great way to stay active instead of being inside. There are two bases about ten to twelve feet apart (I like using a Frisbee or stick to mark each base). A person stands on each base and one person has a ball. The third person, in the middle, tries to tag either base without getting tagged by the ball in the hands of the basemen.

14. GIVE YOUR GARDEN SOME TLC

Once my bulbs are planted, it's time for some garden cleanup. You can leave dried flower heads for the birds to eat the seeds. Once the seeds are gone, cut perennials down to the ground. Remove leaves collected at the base of trees and shrubs. Refresh mulch if desired and spread an organic, granular fertilizer, such as Milorganite. Dried leaves can go into the compost; woody stems can be left out, as they won't decompose as quickly. Want more year-round gardening tips? You can always reference my easy-to-follow trio of gardening guides: Bloom Calendar, Growing Vegetables, and Landscape Design (www.rebeccaplants.com).

15. FIND DESIGNS IN THE STARS

We are familiar with looking for shapes in the clouds; what do you see in the stars? You don't have to know the constellations for this game. Just bundle up and pick a spot in the evening to lay a warm blanket on the ground. Look up at the sky and connect the dots with your fingers to point out to each other the shapes, letters, or numbers you see.

16. MAKE A BEAVER'S HOME

A beaver lives in water, but you don't need water for this pretend game. Use your imagination to create a beaver dam out of sticks. Stack your sticks high just like a beaver to form a dam, but remember to leave an opening at the bottom for the beaver to come and go! A beaver blocks a stream with sticks, and a pond forms behind the dam. If your child wants to pretend to be the beaver, you can create a much larger home of fallen branches, perhaps over a cardboard box with an opening cut out for an entry and exit.

17. MAKE A BIRD'S NEST

Now that the leaves are down, do you see bird's nests in trees? See if you can build a bird's nest with what you find outside: tall dried grass woven together, bits of string, small twigs, maybe even mud. Want to learn about real nests and the birds in your backyard? Join the National Zoo in their Neighborhood Nestwatch program. Learn more at NationalZoo.si.edu.

18. HAVE A WARM SNACKS AND CHARADES PARTY

Invite the neighborhood kids over for hot cocoa and warm cider, s'mores, and popcorn. While the kids are enjoying the snacks, they can play charades outside. Write down on cards ten things, such as animals, that the kids could act out silently that the other children could guess. For example, a cat, dog, bear, bird, worm, snake, rabbit, bat, squirrel, woodpecker, and turtle.

19. SEE THE COLORS OF CAMOUFLAGE

Camouflage is helpful to animals at different times of the year. Look at how the foliage has changed; what type of camouflage helps animals the most now? For example, if grass and brush are now dormant and brown and beige, which animals are harder to see? Squirrels? Bunnies? Deer?

20. PLAY A GAME ON A WALK

My dad loved playing the "Initial Game" in the car on long trips; it's a great activity for walks too or anytime you're outside together and need something to do. The person who goes first says the initials of the person she is thinking of, and the other player(s) can ask questions about the person that require a yes or no answer. For example, the answer to "RPC" would be Rebecca P. Cohen. For younger children, you can play with just the first initial of someone's name and make the sound of that letter.

21. MAKE A FAMILY STEPPING STONE

A wonderful tradition for Thanksgiving is to create a stepping stone each year for the garden. It's easy with a stepping stone kit from a craft store. I find making one stepping stone at a time with everyone pitching in on the decorating easier than worrying about multiple sets of curing concrete. Write the date with a hand print from each of the kids and their names. You can even bring a bit of nature with a leaf print or a mosaic of small, flat rocks.

Find Stillness

Sometimes our lives are so busy that it helps us as parents to take ourselves on a time-out in the open air. Leave your email behind and sneak away for a cup of coffee and sit on a bench and just observe, doing absolutely nothing. Slow your breathing and take deep breaths. Gradually draw your attention to the nature around you, whether the sky, a tree, or a squirrel. Give yourself a good fifteen minutes of stillness, and see how refreshed you feel!

22. MAKE A PATH IN THE FROST

When is your weather due for a temperature at or below thirty-two degrees? Maybe you've already had it. Wake up in the morning and look outside; are there ice crystals on the grass? My younger son loves to put on his boots and coat and run outside with a shovel and make a path or letters in the frost. You could follow each other's footprints too!

23. PREPARE FUN FAMILY GAMES FOR THANKSGIVING

The same relay games that we think of for summer would be fun for a day of family time at Thanksgiving. For example, two people each thread a ribbon through a paper plate that is worn on top of their head. They race to a chair with cotton balls in a bowl, spoon cotton balls on their plates, and race back to the start. The person with the most cotton balls left on their plate wins! What about a two-team race where each person puts on an oversized hat, shirt, necktie, and sunglasses, then removes them for the next person to put on? The team that gets through each player putting on and taking off the four pieces of clothing first wins!

24. "PRETEND YOU'RE A..."

There are fun ways to mimic wildlife outside. For example, wrap tape around your thumb and index finger and be a raccoon trying to hunt for food. Hold chopsticks (with a rubber band around the end or a kids' plastic chopstick helper) to be a praying mantis. Draw a line in chalk on the sidewalk and balance like a squirrel. Curl up like a pill bug. Search for tiny holes in dead logs where woodpeckers might look for insects.

25. LEARN TO PLAY A NEW GAME

Rugby? Cricket? Soccer? Dominos? Chess? What game is new to you that you could learn with your child and have fun together? Are there neighbors that know how to play this game? Ask for help and find a way to learn outside at this time of year.

26. CELEBRATE NATURE AT THANKSGIVING!

In addition to natural décor for the table, there are many ways to incorporate nature into your special day with friends and family. For example, set up a game of kickball for the kids or a scavenger hunt to find objects from nature (e.g., sticks, rocks, acorns, worms, and pinecones). For those not cooking, Rebecca Plants Curiosity Cards are a fun way to pass the time with a favorite relative on the porch. And of course, don't forget to take a stroll after your meal!

27. TAKE BLACK FRIDAY OUTSIDE

Some celebrate the day after Thanksgiving with shopping. How about working off holiday calories with a family activity instead? Jump rope, bike, fish, hike, play football, or sign up for a family fun run. Or engage in an outdoor activity in between your shopping. Go to an outdoor mall and enjoy the fresh air in between ducking in stores.

28. WISH UPON A STAR

Find out when the sun is setting and time how long it takes until you see the first star. Then make a wish! Record your observation in a journal and repeat this experiment for several days. See if you notice a pattern in how long it takes between the sunset and when the first star appears.

29. EXPERIMENT WITH NIGHT VISION

My cousin's daughter Mary taught me a trick from summer camp. When you are enjoying a camp fire, cover one eye and stare at the fire for five to ten minutes. Then un-cover the one eye and quickly cover the other to look into the dark distance. It seems like you are seeing with night vision goggles!

30. LOOK BACK...AND AHEAD

There is one month left in the calendar year. Are you able to get outside for a bit every day? What would make it easier for you? Look back at the list of activities from this and pre-vious months and decide on your favorites; go do one right now! And look ahead—share with one another what you want to make sure you do outside before the end of the year.

december

Celebrate the magic of the season outside.

I used to think that December's shortened daylight hours meant less time for outdoor fun, but now I know better. Early in the morning, my younger son runs in and says softly, "Come look at the beautiful sunrise, Mom!" Through the bare trees, everything is bathed in a warm, pastel light.

On daytime walks, see how many birds and other animals your kids can find. My boys once spotted a gigantic bald eagle's nest that inspired us to put up a bird feeder back home. We made bird food by chopping up nuts, apples, and raisins using plastic knives.

In the twilight, make a campfire and roast s'mores while watching the sunset through the trees. And when darkness falls, the leafless trees allow a clear view for evening star gazing. Take a family stroll through your neighborhood and see how many beautiful twinkle lights you can find; make it a treasure hunt!

After getting outside every day in all kinds of weather, I still hate being cold. But I have learned to find the warmth: bundling up, snuggling with the kids under a blanket, sitting by a campfire. In December, my family likes to seek out organizations that distribute extra warm clothing to people in need. We go through our winter gear and donate jackets, snow pants, and gloves that the boys have outgrown. Talk about a warm feeling!

The winter holidays are filled with excitement. Everything sparkles. From glittery crafts that you make for family and friends to icy frost on the grass, the sunlight catches everything differently. Picking up a Christmas tree is a great family outing. And if you don't want to buy a cut tree, the kids can decorate a tree or shrub in your yard, or even a big indoor houseplant.

On your morning walks, look for beautiful leaves, berries, and other gifts from nature that can be brought home and glued onto paper to make homemade holiday cards. You can also turn one of your best outdoor family photos into a holiday card. Brainstorm with the kids on making homemade gifts for family members. Treasures the children have gathered throughout the year—beach glass, shells, and rocks, for example—can be turned into works of art that any aunt, uncle, or grandparent would appreciate.

December Activities

1. BREATHE EASY

In colder months, those who suffer from outdoor allergies get a break and those who suffer from indoor allergies need to get out! Head outside to enjoy the ability to breathe easily and deeply. If someone has a little cold, that person can breathe out of her mouth. Can you see your breath? Create patterns with it: puffs, a constant stream, and alternating between the two. How else can you change how your breath looks in the cold air?

2. SING IN THE WILDERNESS

Singing and walking outside go together like peanut butter and jelly (except when you're being super-quiet to observe nature). Next time you're walking the kids to school or taking an evening stroll, see if you can get the whole family to join you in a song. And during the holidays, how about finding or even forming a group of singers to go caroling with? You can spread some holiday cheer by ringing your neighbors' doorbells and bursting into song, or bring your merry group to a local nursing home or hospital.

3. JOIN IN THE CHRISTMAS BIRD COUNT!

For over a century, from mid-December to early January, the National Audubon Society has been hosting a Christmas Bird Count. Volunteers from across America—from experienced birders to regular families—are welcome to participate. The results help researchers, biologists, and conservation advocates study the long-term health and status of bird populations across North America. Your kids can report on the number of birds that appear at your own bird feeder, or your family can volunteer to cover a wider area. For more information, check out www.Audubon.org.

4. SHARE YOUR OUTDOOR HOLIDAY TRADITIONS

Ask the people with whom you are celebrating the holidays if they have a special outdoor holiday tradition. The tradition could be something they do every year or just a fond memory of wintertime that they could share either with an outdoor activity, a warm drink, or a dessert that represents that memory for them.

Cheers to Your Outdoor Lifestyle!

You've made it through a year of getting outside more often, every day. An outdoor lifestyle is exactly that: making time to get outside every day to improve your well-being and the well-being of your family. Without fresh air every day, I believe that we are more stressed and less healthy. Daily family time outside keeps us calmer, in shape, and connected to our children. Keep that connection outside alive as your kids grow and their interests change. I've had friends with teenagers tell me that their continued family experiences outside keep their parent-teen relationships strong.

5. HAVE A WARM UP CONTEST

In my house, we love seeing how fast we can do something; take that concept outside and measure how quickly each of you can "warm up." Each person picks their own method: someone may choose jumping jacks; another may run around on the grass; you may hop up and down. When you say "Go!" everyone begins and you look at your watch.

When someone yells, "I'm warm!" you say their time. Next time you go out, switch around activities to experiment with which activity warms each of you up the fastest!

6. CELEBRATE ST. NICHOLAS DAY, OUTDOOR-STYLE

Growing up, on the evening of December 5th, my sisters and I put a pair of our shoes in the front hall. In the morning, we each found an orange and a chocolate bar in them, left by Saint Nick. This European tradition, leaving a surprise gift in children's shoes, led to the tradition of stockings filled by Santa Claus. Put an outdoor twist on this tradition, and if your kids have been good, ask them to put their winter boots by the door and fill each with a homemade coupon for a winter activity they would enjoy, such as outdoor ice skating, tubing, or ice fishing.

7. DISGUISE A WALK AS SOMETHING ELSE

Many times, "Let's go for a walk" doesn't interest my kids one bit. But, if they each bring their favorite ball, we can play catch or kick the ball together along the way. Other times, we'll jog to our ABCs or quiz each other on spelling or funny math problems. If we have to walk the dog, they'll bring their bikes and ride around me in circles while I walk. December in general is an ideal time for evening walks through your neighborhood. See how many beautiful twinkle lights you can find in neighbors' windows. Make it a treasure hunt!

8. SAY GOODNIGHT TO THE MOON

With shorter days, studying the night sky is a fun family activity that doesn't mean the kids have to stay up late! Get to know the upcoming phases of the moon. Then, each evening, the kids can see the moon and say goodnight. MoonConnection. com has a wonderful visual calendar of the moon phases.

9. PAY TRIBUTE TO THE EIGHT NIGHTS OF HANUKKAH

What outdoor traditions could you create eight nights in a row? Light lanterns outside or electric candles in a window? A family walk with hot cocoa for eight evenings? Observing the night sky and how it changes over eight nights? Maybe watching the sunrise or sunset for that many days? Set a goal for what you might like to do outside together for several days in a row and try it!

Showcase Your Photos

Consider a holiday card that is a photo collage of your favorite outdoor memories of the year. Online photo services make it easy with their templates to select several photos to display. The visual reminder of your fun together will not only bring smiles to your faces, but also inspire your family and friends receiving the cards to create their own outdoor lifestyle.

10. MAKE A HOLIDAY TREAT FOR A NEIGHBOR'S DOORSTEP

My friend Nancy's nieces and nephews ask to make this wintertime treat whenever they see her, anytime of year:

cornflakes mixed with melted marshmallows and butter and a little green food coloring, formed into wreaths. Two Red Hots at the top are the ribbon. Turn this into an outdoor tradition by wrapping them, taking a walk, and delivering them to the neighbors.

11. MAKE A CALENDAR OF OUTDOOR MEMORIES

Remember all the pictures that you took of your outdoor family adventures this year? Start a tradition of a calendar that captures those moments in photos each month. Grandparents love these calendars and they are great for your office too. Even better, the kids will love it! My children adore the calendar that they each have hanging in their rooms. They start to associate the months with what we're doing in the pictures.

12. MAKE MORE DÉCOR FROM THE OUTDOORS

In becoming more efficient with my holiday decorating, my husband and I have opted for a faux tree with lights already affixed, but I do love clipping evergreen branches from my yard, such as holly, pine, and magnolia. I place the fresh evergreen branches on the mantle and as a centerpiece on the table, surrounding a glass-enclosed candle.

13. TAKE A MENTAL PICTURE

Bundle up and head out on a mission. Each of you is to find something interesting and spend at least five minutes examining it. Then take the others to your spot and show them what you found; share what you notice about it, and why you like it. Once you head inside, the kids can enjoy a snack and use crayons and paper to draw a picture with a story about what they sat and watched. Hang your child's picture and story in a visible place as a reminder of the fun you have outside together.

14. MAP THE CHANGES IN THE NIGHT SKY

Pick your favorite constellation; for me, it's the Big Dipper. Next, make a map on a piece of paper with your house as the main point of reference. Then, go outside and find the Big Dipper and draw it on your map and mark the date. Whenever you and your child feel like stargazing, bring your map outside with you and draw the position of the Big Dipper, again marking the date. See how its position changes with the seasons.

15. GO FOR ICE CREAM

I was introduced to ice cream in winter when my husband was in law school in Vermont. We'd walk to the local convenience store that had specially discounted pints of Ben and Jerry's ice cream. Head to your nearest ice cream shop and order a scoop to sit and enjoy bundled up on a bench. It's a funny feeling to have ice cream when it's cold out, but it makes for a yummy and silly memory!

16. WALK IN A WINTER WONDERLAND

You might not have snow at Christmastime, but your

township likely has beautiful decorations and a twinkling tree. Head downtown and enjoy the special décor of the season to be together during this special time of year for families. Share what makes this time so meaningful for each of you.

17. GO ON A SLEIGH RIDE

Bring the song "Jingle Bells" to life! Find a farm that offers sleigh rides. Snuggle under a blanket as a family while the driver and horse pull you through the woods. There is nothing quite like the beauty of the woods in wintertime.

18. CREATE A WINTRY LAND OF NARNIA

Remember C. S. Lewis's *The Lion, The Witch, and The Wardrobe*? Have the kids use the yard to create their own winter land of Narnia. Use a bench for the Ice Witch's sleigh, a lamppost for where they meet Mr. Tumnus, and some blankets for the children's fur coats. The children can explore their yard as if it's the new world of Narnia (or any other favorite wintertime story).

19. EXAMINE THE CLOUDS

My mom, an elementary school teacher, loves to teach her fourth and fifth graders about clouds. Cirrus clouds are highest in the sky, wispy, and made of ice crystals. Cumulus clouds are puffy like popcorn or cotton candy and are usually the ones we watch change shape, saying what they look like. Cumulonimbus clouds continue to puff and build, bringing rain and storms in the summer. Stratus clouds are the lowest lying layer of clouds, usually seen when it's foggy and rainy. What clouds do you see?

20. TIRED OF RUNNING? FIND NEW WAYS TO HOP

My neighbor plays this with her three girls, ages three to nine, and I was amazed to see how many creative ways to hop that they came up with. First, have everyone show you the different ways they can hop, skip, or jump. See how long you can keep up the creativity (and exercise!) by calling out the names of animals and insects that hop: frogs, kangaroos, rabbits, grasshoppers, jumping spiders, etc., until you are all laughing hysterically at your hopping creations.

21. WELCOME WINTER

In the Northern Hemisphere, December 21st generally marks the day with the least daylight of the year and the official start of winter. Make it a reason to celebrate! Bring out the warm drinks and glow sticks, build a campfire, roast s'mores, and study the night sky. See how much fun you can have in the dark. Reminisce about your favorite winter memories together in anticipation of the many more you will create this winter season.

22. GO ICE SKATING OUTDOORS

An Internet search can help you find an outdoor ice skating rink, whether man-made or on a frozen pond. Bundling up and lacing up ice skates is a wonderful family activity when together for the holidays. The decorations of outdoor twinkle lights and wreaths make ice skating that much more spectacular; holding each other's hands to stay balanced builds a wonderful bond. The smiles and giggles are endless!

23. CREATE YOUR KING- OR QUEENDOM

You don't have to have a kid to feel like one when playing in the snow. While my friend Darryl's three-year-old daughter Ellie called the six-foot mound of snow left by the snowplow "Ellie's Castle," my sister Marni had her own fairy tale for her birthday, the 23rd of December. Not only did she have a surprise engagement, but she and her betrothed also celebrated with their ninety-pound black lab by romping around their neighborhood, climbing the mountains left by the plows, and even dusting off their sled for multiple runs down a hill, giggling with glee alongside their dog. See how much fun you can have acting like a kid again alongside a special someone.

Celebrate Your Family Favorites!

It's time to poll your family and write down their favorite outdoor memories from the past year. Even simply noting them in the back of this book will start to create amazing momentum for your experiences together in the coming months and years. I absolutely cherish my family's outdoor time together: it is abundant and I never tire of the experiences. I wish you the same for years to come!

24. DECORATE FOR THE BIRDS

Have the kids select a tree that you can see from your window, then decorate it with all the types of bird feeders you can think of! Try pinecones spread with peanut butter (or vegetable shortening) and rolled in popcorn, Cheerios on pipe cleaners, and bagels or bread spread with shortening and dipped in birdseed, sunflower seeds, or any chopped nuts you have on hand. Enjoy watching the birds feast over the next several days.

25. TAKE A TRADITIONAL FAMILY WALK

When my extended family gets together for Christmas dinner, we follow the meal with a traditional walk. Any time there's a family gathering, a nature stroll is a wonderful way to bring people together. We slip into fun and meaningful conversations and walk off those extra calories without even trying.

26. LEARN FROM KWANZAA

A celebration of African American heritage, each of the seven nights of Kwanzaa has a theme: unity, self-determination, collective work and responsibility, cooperative economics, purpose, creativity, and faith. In the morning, with your family, take a vote and pick one of the themes to reflect on for the day. Then, anytime you are outside with your family, whether walking the dog, making a snowman, or sitting on the porch, you can offer your thoughts on the theme of the day and hear what your children have to say.

27. BUILD WITH EMPTY BOXES

Many family members may be huddled over their gifts, fig-uring out how they work and trying them out for the first time. Have the kids take all the empty boxes outside and see what they can build! There is nothing to worry about destroying; the kids can have fun for hours until the boxes are ready to go into the recycling!

28. TAKE A WINTER HIKE

Avoid cabin fever and start burning some holiday calories with a hike at a local park. Look for an easy, one- to two-mile loop so everyone in the family can come. Dress in layers and bring some snacks, water, and binoculars! Winter is a great time for bird watching with the leaves off the trees. Remind anyone new to nature watching that they'll likely see more the quieter they can be on the trail.

29. VISIT TWO MUSEUMS

Why two? You are more likely to park your car in town (pub-lic transportation is even better) and walk around. A chil-dren's or science museum, then a zoo or natural history mu-seum, will be favorites of the kids. You could even make an informal scavenger hunt in town to find five things: a foun-tain, a statue, a garden, a map, and a person wearing a scarf.

30. SEE A FESTIVAL OF LIGHTS

Many towns have a public park or church that has an amaz-ing display of lights through New Year's Eve. Bring your favorite CD of holiday music to play in the car while you tour the lights outside.

31. DANCE OUTSIDE BEFORE BEDTIME!

A wonderful way to celebrate spending a year of outside time together is to crank up the music, twirl glow sticks, decorate with glow-in-the-dark headbands and bracelets, and take the dancing outside! Ring in the New Year (or as late as everyone can stay up) with one last look at the stars before bed. Learn about the night sky at earthsky.org/tonight and make a wish upon a star for your happiest memories outside to be even better next year.

afterword

So What Happens after Every Day Outside?

More of the same, and in a very good way.

Getting outside daily has helped me become very familiar with my family's behavior patterns when it comes to leaving the house. For example, both my kids love exploring new paths and making up games. Gardening is a draw for my younger son; for my older son, it needs to be sports. Seasonal transitions confuse my schedule and make me worried, which makes me think about what is important to me. I've learned how to notice that imbalance in a transition and focus on identifying what I want to be different and changing it. I still hate the feeling of being cold, so I've learned how much clothing I need to wear to stay warm and the same for my kids. Riding bikes and taking walks are my family's instant antidote to stress.

"Forcing us" out of the house even when I don't want to, for example, when it's "too cold" or "too hot," results in fresh air and spontaneous experiences that bring us closer together as a family—every time. How do I know? For one, our smiles and the way we recount our stories to friends and family. Secondly, I see our time outside reflected in my kids' writing at school. The overwhelming majority of their pictures and journaling are about something we've done outside. For example, my older son anticipated with nervousness a three-page writing test he had to complete in school the next day. He much prefers math to reading and writing, so I encouraged him to write about something he loved. After his test, he came home and said with excitement how easy it was because he wrote about the things he loves to do outside.

I am more present, in the moment, and calm with my children when we are outside, and by creating an outdoor lifestyle, I have replaced the mundane with excitement and wonder in our everyday lives. Whether just me with the kids or with my husband too, when we are walking, talking, noticing, and exploring, that is time that I want to bottle up and keep forever—which has happened in my memories of our moments outside together. I can pull an experience from my file in my head at any time, and thinking about the sights, sounds, and smell of a moment with my kids outside diffuses whatever stress I have in the moment. Then that memory easily pulls me to the next experience out of the house with them.

And time outside alone, for me, is my lifeline. Daily walks with the dog, quick bike rides, yoga in the garden, or visits to a nearby stream to listen to the sound of the trickling water melt away my concerns of the day. With some fresh air and movement, I feel grounded, active, and strong, yet relaxed.

So I wish for you the same, that through sharing my experiences you are drawn easily and frequently to creating countless happy memories outside with your family. And that your experiences are not just the precious ones that you will have as you begin this journey, but ones that will develop wonderfully each year, sustaining a priceless family bond.

list of activities

March

April

May

June

August

September

October

December

about the author

Andrea Flanagan

Rebecca P. Cohen is a national gardening and outdoor lifestyle expert and the go-to mom for outdoor activities any time of the year. Rebecca hosts the television series *Get Out of the House*, which shows fun ideas for time outside in every season, and she hosts a radio show of the same name. In addition, she appears on live morning news shows around the country to talk about the how-tos of gardening and living an outdoor lifestyle. Rebecca's work has been featured in *Family Circle*, *Backyard Solutions*, and *Washingtonian* magazines, as well as on Rachael Ray's website Yum-o!, SheKnows.com, and WorkingMother.com.

A former member of the corporate world for fifteen years and a mom of two young boys, Rebecca started her company, Rebecca Plants, LLC, in 2007 to pursue her passion for inspiring others to garden, be outside, and improve their well-being. Rebecca's unique products along with her inspiring videos and television show help families have fun outside and see how easy it is to fit an outdoor lifestyle into a busy schedule. Every day, Rebecca receives emails from appreciative parents and grandparents who have been inspired to get out of the house and improve their well-being, thanks to Rebecca Plants, LLC. In 2010 Rebecca was the youngest inventor to be featured in the book *The Right Sisters: Women Inventors Tell Their Stories*, by Julia Rhodes, for the pursuit of her life's work to improve the well-being of others through simple gardening and outdoor activities.

Rebecca is also an advocate with corporations and public schools for the funding of school gardens and outdoor learning. She has led thousands of children in lessons outside to inspire hands-on learning, healthy lifestyles, and more outdoor lessons in the curriculum. In 2009 she was awarded Volunteer of the Year by the Arlington Outdoor Education Association in Arlington, Virginia, which hosts nine thousand public school students every year at its Phoebe Hall Knipling Outdoor Lab.

Rebecca is also a spokesmom for the National Wildlife Federation's Be Out There movement. For more information, visit RebeccaPlants.com.

additional resources from rebecca plants, LLC

Curiosity Cards

(www.rebeccaplants.com/cards.asp) A great companion tool to this book, Rebecca Plants Curiosity Cards are a portable set of fifty open-ended questions on a ring that can be used anywhere to make the most of your family time together.

Growing Vegetables: The Basics

(www.rebeccaplants.com/growingvegetables.asp) This two-page guide has everything you need to get started with my top five picks for the easiest vegetables to grow and my top five picks for the easiest herbs to grow.

Bloom Calendar

(www.rebeccaplants.com/bloomcal.asp) This two-page guide explains and gives pictures of the most fail-proof perennials, when they bloom, and how long they bloom to achieve season-long color. Plus, it contains countless tips for garden care.

Landscape Design

(www.rebeccaplants.com/landscapedesign.asp) This two-page

guide is like having your own gardening coach help you b̶c̶
and lay out your flowers, trees, and shrubs for the best look.

50 Outdoor Activities for Busy Families

(www.rebeccaplants.com/outdoorliving.asp) This two-page
guide features simple activities to have on hand for fun
year-round.

Outdoor Classrooms: The Basics

(www.rebeccaplants.com/outdoorliving.asp#classroom)
This two-page guide covers the process of how to start a
learning garden and gives ideas for outdoor lessons for
every season.